29.95

Golfing
NORTHERN CALIFORNIA

Golfing
NORTHERN CALIFORNIA

TIM KEYSER

PELICAN PUBLISHING COMPANY
Gretna 1991

Library of Congress Cataloging-in-Publication Data

Keyser, Tim.
    Golfing northern California / by Tim Keyser.
       p. cm.
    ISBN 0–88289–745–4
    1. Golf courses—California, Northern—Directories.
    2. California, Northern—Description and travel—Guide-books.
    I. Title.
    GV982.C23K48 1990
    796.352'06'8794—dc20   90–32032
                                                 CIP

*Jacket photograph: Pine Mountain
Lake Country Club in Groveland*

Photographs by Tim Keyser

Maps by Michael Forsythe

Manufactured in Hong Kong

Published by Pelican Publishing Company, Inc.
1101 Monroe Street, Gretna, Louisiana 70053

CONTENTS

INTRODUCTION

This book is a practical guide for playing the public 18-hole golf courses of Northern California. Also, it contains information on quality and value, and assorted facts that allow you to compare your local course with all other courses in Northern California.

It was not easy locating all the golf courses as there are no other complete golfing guides in publication. For the purpose of this guidebook, it includes all *known* public, 18-hole regulation (par 68 and above) golf courses.

For a course to qualify as public, anyone may play there without any stipulations other than paying a green fee and making a tee time. Courses that are open to members only or guests of a resort, that are closed to the public on weekends, certain times of the day, or have other restrictions are not included in this golfing guide.

The area covered in this book is all of California from the town of Tulare in the south to the Oregon/California border in the north. There are 112 golf courses in this area.

If there is a public course in Northern California that meets these criteria but is *not* listed in this book, please accept my apologies and notify me of my inadvertent omission.

I have been playing golf since the 1960s. Raised in California, I have competed in this sport on the high school, collegiate, and professional levels. Now living in Northern California, I have played more than three hundred golf courses nationwide.

I will shoot scratch golf and thoroughly enjoy playing new courses. I like challenging courses, but fun and beautiful courses are also very enjoyable. In other words, I like playing a variety of different courses.

In researching this golf guide, I have experienced the ultimate in golfing pleasure. Having played every public, 18-hole, regulation golf course in Northern California, I definitely have the firsthand knowledge for comparing golf courses. I have based my evaluations on this knowledge and experience.

The ratings in this guidebook are my own opinions. Before any golf course was researched or rated, worksheets were drawn up indicating what specific information was needed on each course. This book was *not* done from memory. During research, more than 1,050 hours were spent and in excess of 14,000 miles driven to gather the enclosed information. Accurate and detailed notes were kept.

Each golf course was visited, played, and photographed (more than 3,300 pictures with two different cameras). Each course was rated before the next course was played. After all the golf courses were finished, some changes were necessary. Now a complete picture was at hand which allowed accurate comparisons for quality, value, scenery, difficulty, condition, etc.

QUALITY RATING SYSTEM

The quality rating system is used to determine the "Quality of Play" for each golf course. A maximum of 100 points is possible using nine different rating criteria. These criteria and their possible point values are listed below:

	POOR	BELOW AVERAGE	AVERAGE	GOOD	VERY GOOD	OUTSTANDING
OVERALL APPEAL	0	3	6	9	12	15
DESIGN & VARIETY	0	3	6	9	12	15
SCENERY	0	3	6	9	12	15
OVERALL DIFFICULTY	0	2	4	6	8	10
GREENS DIFFICULTY	0	2	4	6	8	10
OVERALL CONDITION	0	2	4	6	8	10
GREENS CONDITION	0	2	4	6	8	10
HAZARDS	0	2	4	6	8	10
COSMETICS	0	1	2	3	4	5
TOTAL	0	20	40	60	80	100

The quality of a golf course is determined by the number of points it receives. Following is the list of quality categories and number of points needed to achieve them.

Outstanding	92–100	points
Very Good	80– 91	points
Good	60– 79	points
Average	40– 59	points
Below Average	20– 39	points
Poor	0– 19	points

For example, if a golf course has a quality rating of 73 it would be a *good* golf course to play. If a golf course has a quality rating of 29, it would be a *below average* course to play.

If you look closely at the quality rating system you will notice that different criteria have different point values. For instance, if a golf course has *outstanding scenery*, it will receive 15 points in that category. If the golf course has *outstanding overall difficulty*, it will receive only 10 points. And, if the golf course has outstanding cosmetics, it will receive only 5 points. The explanation for this is simple. In determining the quality of play at a golf course, I feel scenery is more important than difficulty and cosmetics is the least important of all the criteria. Each golf course is rated against all other public, 18-hole, regulation courses in Northern California. Continue on for the explanation of each criteria.

OVERALL APPEAL: This criterion critiques the total experience and pleasure derived from the golf course. Almost everything was taken into consideration, from the condition of the course, location, scenery, difficulty, etc. Weather conditions or the price of the green fees were *not* taken into consideration. The course did not have to be extremely difficult or in magnificent condition to get a high rating. The more enjoyable the course, the more points it received.

DESIGN AND VARIETY: This rating evaluates the design of the golf course. If the course had most of its holes looking the same, it got a lower rating. Golf courses with holes that are long, short, wide, narrow, dogleg lefts, dogleg rights, easy holes, and difficult holes received a high rating. Golf courses with "tricked-up" holes making it unfair for golfers received lower ratings. Also, courses that have a mixture of strategic, penal, and heroic (gambler's) holes were awarded more points.

SCENERY: This criterion critiques scenery both on and off the golf course. Panoramic views, city views, trees, lakes, and homes can all be highly scenic. A golf course can be located in a beautiful location, but on-course distractions such as brown dirt, run-down buildings, piles of trash, unmaintained lakes, and other "eyesores" would reduce its points in this category.

OVERALL DIFFICULTY: This rating deals with the difficulty of the course *before* you get on the green. A lot of things were taken into consideration including length of the course, width of the fairways, severity of the holes, etc. Weather conditions such as wind were not taken into consideration, and neither were maintenance conditions of the course. In other words, the tougher it is to shoot low scores, the more points the golf course received in this category.

GREENS DIFFICULTY: This criterion lets you know how difficult the greens are to putt. Greens that are flat, little circles did not get very many points. These greens are boring with almost every putt looking the same. Greens that are large and undulating received a higher rating. In other words, greens that make you "think" got the highest ratings.

OVERALL CONDITION: This rating critiques the maintenance of the *entire* golf course (other than the greens). Fairways, tee boxes, roughs, trees, lakes, hazards, bunkers, and all other areas of the course are part of this criterion. Temporary conditions such as water build-up after a heavy rain, construction works, etc., were not taken into consideration and did *not* detract from the points the course received. Old divots in the fairways that were not replaced reduced the points the course received.

GREENS CONDITION: This criterion evaluates the maintenance of the greens. For a golf course to receive the most points in this category, the greens must hold, putt true, have very little bounce to the putts, and be free of weeds. Temporary conditions such as top-dressing and so on were not taken into consideration and no points were deducted. Old, unrepaired ball marks brought down the condition rating of the greens. It should be the responsibility of the management *and* the golfer to repair ball marks.

HAZARDS: This rating critiques the quality and quantity of all hazards on the golf course. As a rule, if it is easy to get into hazards and difficult to recover from them, then the golf course received more points. Hazards that were non-existent, did not come into play, or were easy to recover from were not rated very high. Also, the variety of trees, water bunkers, creeks, etc., were taken into consideration.

COSMETICS: This criterion considers all the "little extras" management provides the golfer to make his/her round more enjoyable. As an example: nice cart paths, plenty of drinking fountains, benches, hole-description signs on tee boxes, fountains in the lakes, decorated flower beds, and con-toured fairways are just a few of the "finishing touches" considered here. The maintenance conditions of these cosmetics were also judged. Golf courses with plenty of cosmetics tend to be of country-club caliber.

When you look at the quality rating system closely, you will find that golf courses do not change much. *Overall appeal* and *cosmetics* will change very little in most cases. *Design and variety, scenery, overall difficulty, greens difficulty,* and *hazards* almost never change.

Overall condition and *greens condition* are the criteria that are the most likely to change. Management turnovers, change in the amount of money a golf course has to spend, and pride of both the players and management will alter the maintenance conditions of a course. However, over the years you will find that even these changes will have little impact. In other words, at any given time greens might go from *good* to *average* or from *good* to *very good.* It is highly unlikely that greens conditions will go from *below average* to *outstanding* or vice versa.

For those golf courses that have improved their facilities since the ratings were made, congratulations! For those courses that decreased their quality, hopefully you will improve them in the near future.

A complete list of Northern California's quality ranking follows the section of golf course listings.

VALUE RATING SYSTEM

The value rating system is used to determine the quality of golf you will receive for the money you have to pay. This system uses the school system of grading. Listed below is the value rating.

A	=	**EXCELLENT**	value
B	=	**GOOD**	value
C	=	**AVERAGE**	value
D	=	**BELOW AVERAGE**	value
F	=	**POOR**	value

Since golf courses vary in quality and charge different green fees, I devised a formula to compare value for all of Northern California's public, 18-hole regulation golf courses. To be fair to all courses involved, all courses were called on the same day, and current green fees at that time were used to calculate value ratings.

Naturally, the better the golf course is, the more money it should be able to charge and still receive a high rating value. However, there is a point where golf courses charge too much in relation to other courses, no matter how good their course is. The quality factor used in this value rating formula allows a golf course to charge a higher green fee to maintain its quality. The quality factors are listed below:

		QUALITY FACTOR
OUTSTANDING	golf course	**x 6**
VERY GOOD	golf course	**x 5**
GOOD	golf course	**x 4**
AVERAGE	golf course	**x 3**
BELOW AVERAGE	golf course	**x 2**
POOR	golf course	**x 1**

For example: If a golf course has a quality rating of 73, and a weekday green fee of $12, then the value formula would look like this:

QUALITY RATING ÷ WEEKDAY GREEN FEE = VALUE POINTS x QUALITY FACTOR = **VALUE RATING**

| 73 | ÷ | $12 | = | 6.083 | x | 4 | = | **24.3** |

Another example: If a golf course has a quality rating of 64, and a weekday green fee of $34, then the value formula would look like this:

QUALITY RATING ÷ WEEKDAY GREEN FEE = VALUE POINTS x QUALITY FACTOR = **VALUE RATING**

| 64 | ÷ | $34 | = | 1.882 | x | 4 | = | **7.5** |

One more example: If a golf course has a quality rating of 31, and a weekday green fee of $9, then the value formula would look like this:

QUALITY RATING ÷ WEEKDAY GREEN FEE = VALUE POINTS x QUALITY FACTOR = **VALUE RATING**

| 31 | ÷ | $9 | = | 3.444 | x | 2 | = | **6.9** |

After all golf courses were rated for value, they were ranked from the very best value to the worst value in Northern California.

TOP	**9%**	received an	**A**	value
NEXT	**21%**	received a	**B**	value
NEXT	**40%**	received a	**C**	value
NEXT	**21%**	received a	**D**	value
BOTTOM	**9%**	received an	**F**	value

For a listing of all 112 public, 18-hole, regulation golf courses and their value ratings, please turn to the end of the book.

Hopefully when golf course managements realize they are offering their golfers a good or excellent value, they will keep up the good work. On the other hand, for those courses that received low value rankings, hopefully they will improve in the near future.

☐	☐	■	☐	☐	☐
Poor	Below Average	Average	Good	Very Good	Outstanding

Quality Rating	**41**
Value Rating	**C**

SAMPLE GOLF COURSE LISTING

Address
City, Zip
Telephone
Ownership   Type of golf course
Weekday Fee
Weekend Fee   ➤   Rates of golf course
Twilight Fee

Men's Par
Men's Yardage
Men's Rating   NCGA Rating
Women's Par
Women's Yardage
Women's Rating
Championship
    Yardage
Championship
    Rating

Course Map or Photo

QUALITY OF PLAY

OVERALL APPEAL	Average	6	of possible	15
DESIGN & VARIETY	Average	6	of possible	15
SCENERY	Below Average	3	of possible	15
OVERALL DIFFICULTY	Good	6	of possible	10
GREENS DIFFICULTY	Good	6	of possible	10
OVERALL CONDITION	Average	4	of possible	10
GREENS CONDITION	Average	4	of possible	10
HAZARDS	Average	4	of possible	10
COSMETICS	Average	2	of possible	5
TOTAL	**Average**	**41**	**of possible**	**100**

QUALITY RATING

Description   1. Width of fairways, type of trees and general terrain
        2. General location and surroundings
        3. Type of hazards
        4. Special notes
        5. TOP TEN LISTINGS (if any)

QUALITY AND VALUE RANKINGS
for Northern California

Clubhouse Facilities   Bold letters indicate the "quality" of the facilities—**POOR, FAIR, GOOD, OR EXCELLENT**

Practice Facilities   Bold letters indicate the "quality" of the facilities—**POOR, FAIR, GOOD, OR EXCELLENT**

Who Should Play   The type of golfer this course is best suited for

Walkability   The degree of difficulty when walking the course—Easy, Moderate, or Difficult

**Directional Map
(not drawn to scale)**

Directions   *Easy directions to the golf course. Remember, mileage is only approximate.*

Golfing
NORTHERN CALIFORNIA

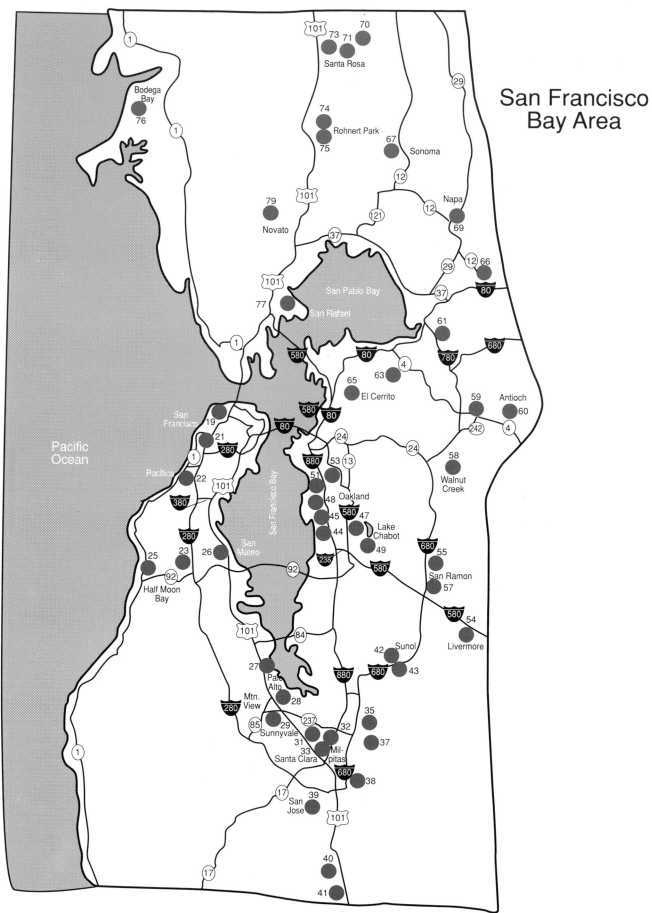

San Francisco Bay Area

Numbered dots indicate the page number where the golf course is described.

SAN FRANCISCO BAY AREA

The San Francisco Bay Area offers the most diversified quality, value, and geographic types of golf courses in Northern California. This zone covers an area from the Pacific Ocean in the west, to Livermore Valley in the east, Santa Rosa in the north, to south of San Jose at Coyote. Some courses are seaside courses. Some are tucked nicely in the coastal foothills and others are in the very heart of large, metropolitan areas. A few golf courses are very well maintained while others are not. Some are hilly, while others are flat.

Weather conditions in this zone will vary from season to season and from location to location. Golf is enjoyed on a year-round basis. Usually, in late winter and early fall the foothills are beautifully green and lush while in the summer they turn brown. Moderate rainfall means many sunny days for golfing. Weather along the coast can be quite cool while the inland valleys can be quite warm. Golf courses located along the ocean or bay can sometimes be very windy.

Municipal/county courses are usually inexpensive, but sometimes crowded. Allow plenty of time for play. Weekends you should make tee times prior to playing. With a few exceptions, these courses are not maintained as well as they should be. Dress code is generally informal.

Most independent courses are moderately priced and sometimes crowded. Maintenance conditions vary from poor to outstanding. Some of these courses are very relaxed and casual while others are very upscale and formal. There are no public resort golf courses in the San Francisco Bay Area.

☐	☐	■	☐	☐	☐
Poor	Below Average	Average	Good	Very Good	Outstanding

Quality Rating	**40**
Value Rating	**C**

LINCOLN PARK GOLF COURSE

Address   3139 Clement Street
City, Zip   San Francisco, 94121
Telephone   (415) 221–9911
Ownership   Municipal
Weekday Fee $8
Weekend Fee $12
Twilight Fee $4

Men's Par   69
Men's Yardage   5311
Men's Rating   —
Women's Par   72
Women's Yardage   5311
Women's Rating   —
Championship
    Yardage   —
Championship
    Rating   —

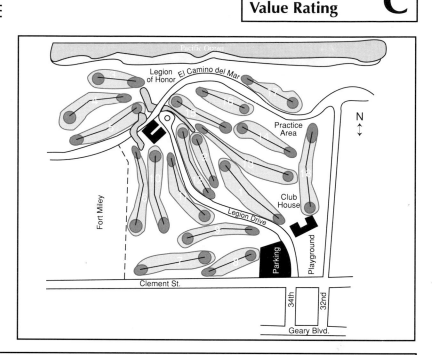

OVERALL APPEAL	Average	6	of possible	15
DESIGN & VARIETY	Below Average	3	of possible	15
SCENERY	Outstanding	15	of possible	15
OVERALL DIFFICULTY	Below Average	2	of possible	10
GREENS DIFFICULTY	Average	4	of possible	10
OVERALL CONDITION	Below Average	2	of possible	10
GREENS CONDITION	Below Average	2	of possible	10
HAZARDS	Good	6	of possible	10
COSMETICS	Poor	0	of possible	5
TOTAL	**Average**	**40**	**of possible**	**100**

Description   Located in Lincoln Park, this course sits high above the Pacific Ocean with grand views of the Golden Gate Bridge from the 17th hole. Narrow to medium-wide fairways bordered by mature cypress, pine, and eucalyptus trees provide most of the hazards. This course is relatively short with the average par 4 being about 300 yards. However, majestic scenery on and off the course almost makes you forget about golf. 6th BEST SCENERY

QUALITY RANKING 89th   VALUE RANKING 53rd
Clubhouse Facilities   FAIR   Pro shop, snack bar, full
    bar, banquet
Practice Facilities   POOR   Putting green

Who Should Play   High-handicappers or those looking for scenery
Walkability   Difficult

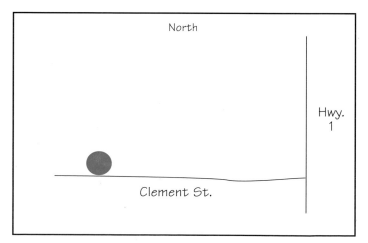

Directions   *From Highway 1: Go west on Clement Street to the golf course.*

19

Quality Rating **81**

Value Rating **A**

HARDING PARK GOLF COURSE

Address   Harding Park Road
City, Zip   San Francisco, 94117
Telephone   (415) 664–4690
Ownership   Municipal
Weekday Fee $10
Weekend Fee $15
Twilight Fee $5

Men's Par   72
Men's Yardage   6637
Men's Rating   70.8
Women's Par   73
Women's Yardage   6156
Women's Rating   73.0
Championship
   Yardage   —
Championship
   Rating   —

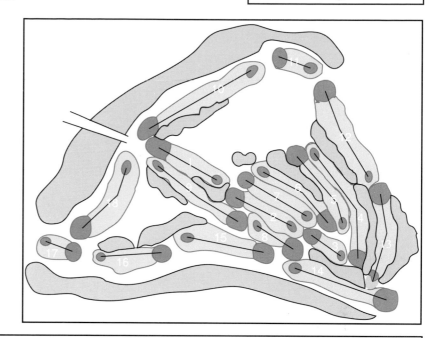

OVERALL APPEAL	Outstanding	15	of possible	15
DESIGN & VARIETY	Outstanding	15	of possible	15
SCENERY	Outstanding	15	of possible	15
OVERALL DIFFICULTY	Very Good	8	of possible	10
GREENS DIFFICULTY	Good	6	of possible	10
OVERALL CONDITION	Good	6	of possible	10
GREENS CONDITION	Good	6	of possible	10
HAZARDS	Very Good	8	of possible	10
COSMETICS	Average	2	of possible	5
TOTAL	**Very Good**	**81**	**of possible**	**100**

Description   Located in Harding Park, this course is bordered on three sides by Lake Merced. Magnificently mature cypress trees border medium to wide fairways. Most holes are flat with a few undulations. Extremely pleasant to play and challenging at the same time. Changing weather sometimes makes for interesting moods on the course. Some holes have beautiful views of Lake Merced. Fairways are lush green in appearance. 8th BEST SCENERY 5th BEST "FUN COURSE"

QUALITY RANKING   17th   VALUE RANKING   1st
Clubhouse Facilities   FAIR   Pro shop, snack bar, full bar
Practice Facilities   FAIR   2 putting greens, driving range
Who Should Play   Everyone

Walkability   Easy

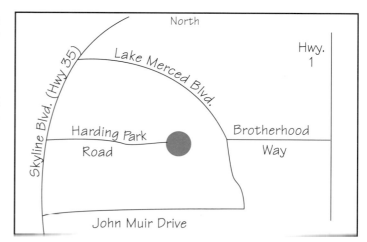

Directions   *Take Skyline Boulevard (Highway 35) south and exit east on Harding Park Road to the golf course.*

☐	☐	■	☐	☐	☐
Poor	Below Average	Average	Good	Very Good	Outstanding

SHARP PARK GOLF COURSE

Address	Sharp Park Road
City, Zip	Pacifica, 94044
Telephone	(415) 355-2862
Ownership	Municipal
Weekday Fee	$8
Weekend Fee	$12
Twilight Fee	$4

Men's Par	72
Men's Yardage	6283
Men's Rating	69.3
Women's Par	74
Women's Yardage	—
Women's Rating	—
Championship Yardage	—
Championship Rating	—

OVERALL APPEAL	Good	9	of possible	15
DESIGN & VARIETY	Good	9	of possible	15
SCENERY	Outstanding	15	of possible	15
OVERALL DIFFICULTY	Good	6	of possible	10
GREENS DIFFICULTY	Average	4	of possible	10
OVERALL CONDITION	Below Average	2	of possible	10
GREENS CONDITION	Average	4	of possible	10
HAZARDS	Good	6	of possible	10
COSMETICS	Poor	0	of possible	5
TOTAL	**Average**	**55**	**of possible**	**100**

Description   Located next to the ocean, but no ocean views because of a man-made levee. However, beautiful, mature cypress and pine trees border narrow to medium-wide fairways making it quite scenic. This course is flat with a few small hills. Some challenging holes make for interesting play. With more emphasis on maintenance it could be a much better golf course.

QUALITY RANKING   51st   VALUE RANKING   26th
Clubhouse Facilities   FAIR   Pro shop, snack bar, full bar, coffee shop
Practice Facilities   POOR   Putting green

Who Should Play   Everyone

Walkability   Moderate

North   Pacifica

Hwy. 1

Sharp Park Road

Directions   *Go south on Highway 1 and exit west on Sharp Park Road to golf course.*

	Poor	Below Average	Average	Good	Very Good	Outstanding

CRYSTAL SPRINGS GOLF CLUB

Address	6650 Golf Course Drive
City, Zip	Burlingame, 94010
Telephone	(415) 342–0603
Ownership	Independent
Weekday Fee	$25
Weekend Fee	$30
Twilight Fee	$20
Men's Par	72
Men's Yardage	6321
Men's Rating	69.9
Women's Par	72
Women's Yardage	5890
Women's Rating	71.2
Championship Yardage	6683
Championship Rating	71.1

OVERALL APPEAL	Outstanding	15	of possible	15
DESIGN & VARIETY	Outstanding	15	of possible	15
SCENERY	Outstanding	15	of possible	15
OVERALL DIFFICULTY	Very Good	8	of possible	10
GREENS DIFFICULTY	Good	6	of possible	10
OVERALL CONDITION	Good	6	of possible	10
GREENS CONDITION	Good	6	of possible	10
HAZARDS	Very Good	8	of possible	10
COSMETICS	Below Average	1	of possible	5
TOTAL	**Very Good**	**80**	**of possible**	**100**

Description Interstate Highway 280 borders one side while mountainous terrain borders the other side. Very hilly. Many holes tend to fall off steeply on one side, making course management a must. Narrow to medium-wide fairways bordered by mature pine and eucalyptus trees. Lots of elevated tee boxes and greens provide interesting holes. Also, there are many beautiful views of the Santa Cruz Mountains and Crystal Springs Reservoir.

QUALITY RANKING   21st   VALUE RANKING   47th
Clubhouse Facilities   FAIR   Pro shop, snack bar, full bar, banquet
Practice Facilities   FAIR   Putting green, night driving range
Who Should Play   Everyone

Walkability   Difficult

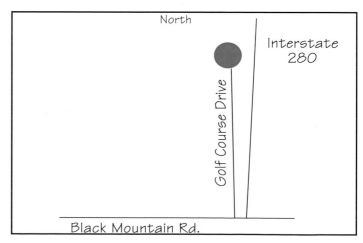

Directions   *From I280: Exit west on Black Mountain Road. Go north on Golf Course Drive to golf course.*

Poor	Below Average	Average	Good	Very Good	Outstanding
□	□	□	□	■	□

Quality Rating	**90**
Value Rating	**C**

HALF MOON BAY GOLF LINKS

Address	2000 Fairway Drive
City, Zip	Half Moon Bay, 94019
Telephone	(415) 726–4438
Ownership	Independent
Weekday Fee	$40
Weekend Fee	$55
Twilight Fee	$25

Men's Par	72
Men's Yardage	6422
Men's Rating	71.0
Women's Par	72
Women's Yardage	5710
Women's Rating	73.0
Championship Yardage	7116
Championship Rating	74.5

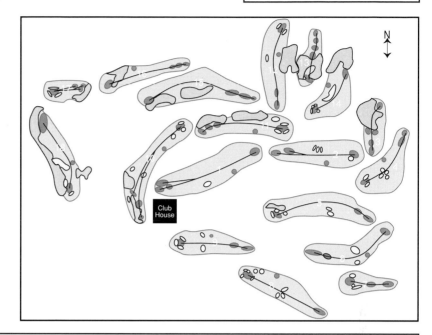

OVERALL APPEAL	Outstanding	15	of possible	15
DESIGN & VARIETY	Outstanding	15	of possible	15
SCENERY	Outstanding	15	of possible	15
OVERALL DIFFICULTY	Outstanding	10	of possible	10
GREENS DIFFICULTY	Very Good	8	of possible	10
OVERALL CONDITION	Very Good	8	of possible	10
GREENS CONDITION	Good	6	of possible	10
HAZARDS	Outstanding	10	of possible	10
COSMETICS	Good	3	of possible	5
TOTAL	**Very Good**	**90**	**of possible**	**100**

Description   Located in an up-scale housing development with most holes weaving around beautiful homes, this course is exciting and challenging. Many bunkers, water, barrancas, and bluffs provide exceptional hazards. Most holes have gentle hills with medium to wide fairways bordered by young to mature pine trees. The 18th hole is spectacular with a panoramic view of the ocean. 8th BEST "FUN COURSE" 6th MOST DIFFICULT COURSE 10th BEST DESIGN 10th BEST HAZARDS 2nd BEST FINISHING HOLE 5th BEST SCORECARD

QUALITY RANKING   10th   VALUE RANKING   72nd
Clubhouse Facilities   GOOD   Pro shop, snack bar, full bar
Practice Facilities   POOR   Putting green
Who Should Play   Everyone
Walkability   Carts are mandatory

Directions   *Go south on Highway 1 about 2 miles. Exit west on Fairway Drive to the golf course.*

Poor	Below Average	Average	Good	Very Good	Outstanding

Quality Rating	28
Value Rating	D

SAN MATEO GOLF COURSE

Address	Coyote Point Drive
City, Zip	San Mateo, 94401
Telephone	(415) 347–1461
Ownership	Municipal
Weekday Fee	$8
Weekend Fee	$10
Twilight Fee	$6

Men's Par	70
Men's Yardage	5496
Men's Rating	64.7
Women's Par	72
Women's Yardage	5451
Women's Rating	69.7
Championship Yardage	5853
Championship Rating	66.5

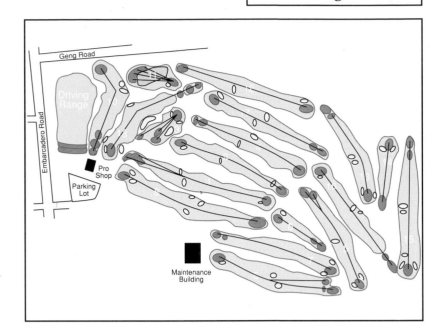

OVERALL APPEAL	Below Average	3	of possible	15
DESIGN & VARIETY	Below Average	3	of possible	15
SCENERY	Below Average	3	of possible	15
OVERALL DIFFICULTY	Average	4	of possible	10
GREENS DIFFICULTY	Average	4	of possible	10
OVERALL CONDITION	Below Average	2	of possible	10
GREENS CONDITION	Average	4	of possible	10
HAZARDS	Average	4	of possible	10
COSMETICS	Below Average	1	of possible	5
TOTAL	**Below Average**	**28**	**of possible**	**100**

Description   Located adjacent to Coyote Point County Park this course is flat, with medium-wide fairways bordered by middle-aged eucalyptus trees. Not much imagination in design and most holes play rather short. Some power lines run through the course taking away some of the beauty of nearby Coyote Point County Park.

QUALITY RANKING 103rd VALUE RANKING 95th
Clubhouse Facilities   FAIR   Pro shop, full bar, coffee shop
Practice Facilities   POOR   3 putting greens, driving net
Who Should Play   Those looking for convenience

Walkability   Easy

Directions   *From Highway 101: Exit east on Peninsula Avenue to golf course.*

26

Poor	Below Average	Average	Good	Very Good	Outstanding
☐	☐	☐	■	☐	☐

Quality Rating **65**

Value Rating **A**

PALO ALTO MUNICIPAL GOLF COURSE

Address	1875 Embarcadero Road
City, Zip	Palo Alto, 94303
Telephone	(415) 856–0881
Ownership	Municipal
Weekday Fee	$9
Weekend Fee	$12.50
Twilight Fee	$6.50

Men's Par	72
Men's Yardage	6525
Men's Rating	70.7
Women's Par	73
Women's Yardage	5852
Women's Rating	73.2
Championship Yardage	6854
Championship Rating	72.2

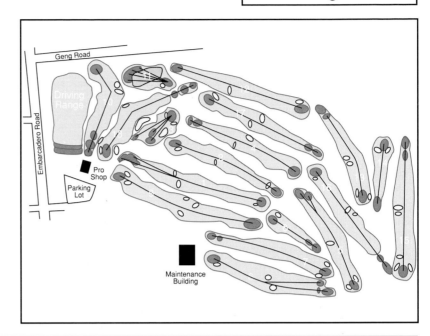

OVERALL APPEAL	Good	9	of possible	15
DESIGN & VARIETY	Good	9	of possible	15
SCENERY	Average	6	of possible	15
OVERALL DIFFICULTY	Very Good	8	of possible	10
GREENS DIFFICULTY	Good	6	of possible	10
OVERALL CONDITION	Very Good	8	of possible	10
GREENS CONDITION	Outstanding	10	of possible	10
HAZARDS	Good	6	of possible	10
COSMETICS	Good	3	of possible	5
TOTAL	**Good**	**65**	**of possible**	**100**

Description   Next to the Palo Alto airport, this course is flat with medium to wide fairways bordered by young to middle-aged trees. Bunkers and some water provide the majority of the hazards. An excellent municipal operation that shows a lot of pride. This course is challenging for the avid golfer and enjoyable for the high-handicapper. However, many holes tend to be similar. 5th BEST OVERALL CONDITION 6th BEST GREENS CONDITION 8th BEST PRACTICE FACILITIES 8th BEST SCORECARD

QUALITY RANKING   39th   VALUE RANKING   6th
Clubhouse Facilities   FAIR Pro shop, snack bar, full bar
Practice Facilities   EXCELLENT Putting green, driving range
Who Should Play Everyone

Walkability   Easy

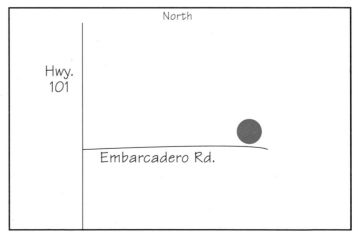

Directions   *From Highway 101: Exit east on Embarcadero Road to the golf course.*

Poor	Below Average	Average	Good	Very Good	Outstanding
☐	☐	☐	■	☐	☐

Quality Rating **69**

Value Rating **C**

SHORELINE GOLF COURSE

Address	2600 Stierlin Road
City, Zip	Mountain View, 94043
Telephone	(415) 969–2041
Ownership	Independent
Weekday Fee	$25
Weekend Fee	$29
Twilight Fee	$13

Men's Par	72
Men's Yardage	6235
Men's Rating	69.0
Women's Par	72
Women's Yardage	5488
Women's Rating	70.2
Championship Yardage	6763
Championship Rating	71.9

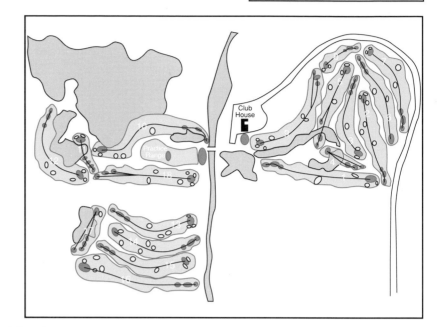

OVERALL APPEAL	Good	9	of possible	15
DESIGN & VARIETY	Very Good	12	of possible	15
SCENERY	Average	6	of possible	15
OVERALL DIFFICULTY	Very Good	8	of possible	10
GREENS DIFFICULTY	Outstanding	10	of possible	10
OVERALL CONDITION	Very Good	8	of possible	10
GREENS CONDITION	Good	6	of possible	10
HAZARDS	Good	6	of possible	10
COSMETICS	Very Good	4	of possible	5
TOTAL	**Good**	**69**	**of possible**	**100**

Description This course is relatively flat with very large mounds surrounding the greens and alongside the fairways. There are plenty of large, contoured bunkers that are attractive but really do not come into play. Medium to wide fairways are bordered by young trees. Some holes have water. Interesting course to play with some views of the Shoreline Amphitheater. Greens are extremely large with many undulations. 6th BEST OVERALL CONDITION 10th MOST DIFFICULT GREENS 10th BEST SCORECARD

QUALITY RANKING   35th   VALUE RANKING   75th
Clubhouse Facilities   GOOD Pro shop, snack bar

Practice Facilities   GOOD Putting green, driving range, chipping green, 2 bunkers
Who Should Play Everyone

Walkability Easy

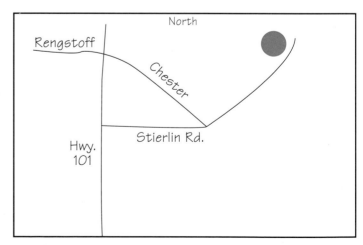

Directions *From Highway 101: Exit east on Stierlin Road to the golf course.*

| Poor | Below Average | Average | Good | Very Good | Outstanding |

SUNNYVALE MUNICIPAL GOLF COURSE

Address	605 Macara Avenue
City, Zip	Sunnyvale, 94086
Telephone	(408) 738–3666
Ownership	Municipal
Weekday Fee	$9.50
Weekend Fee	$13
Twilight Fee	$6

Men's Par	70
Men's Yardage	5744
Men's Rating	67.0
Women's Par	71
Women's Yardage	5176
Women's Rating	67.0
Championship Yardage	6150
Championship Rating	68.0

OVERALL APPEAL	Average	6	of possible	15
DESIGN & VARIETY	Average	6	of possible	15
SCENERY	Average	6	of possible	15
OVERALL DIFFICULTY	Good	6	of possible	10
GREENS DIFFICULTY	Average	4	of possible	10
OVERALL CONDITION	Good	6	of possible	10
GREENS CONDITION	Average	4	of possible	10
HAZARDS	Good	6	of possible	10
COSMETICS	Average	2	of possible	5
TOTAL	**Average**	**46**	**of possible**	**100**

Description   Flat, with most holes having wide fairways bordered by young to middle-aged pine and eucalyptus trees. This course is surrounded by commercial buildings on one side and Highway 101 on the other. There are plenty of wide, sweeping doglegs and a few holes are much more narrow with larger trees. Some very strategically placed water makes a few holes interesting to play.

QUALITY RANKING   75th   VALUE RANKING   55th
Clubhouse Facilities   GOOD   Pro shop, coffee shop, full bar, banquets
Practice Facilities   POOR   Putting green

Who Should Play   Everyone

Walkability   Easy

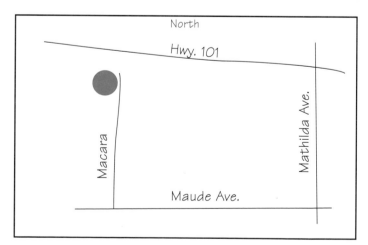

Directions   *From Highway 101: Exit south on Mathilda Avenue and go about 1/2 mile. Go west on Maude Avenue about 1 mile. Go north on Macara Avenue to the golf course.*

SANTA CLARA GOLF & TENNIS CLUB

			▮			Quality Rating **67**
						Value Rating **B**

SANTA CLARA GOLF & TENNIS CLUB

Address	2501 Talluto Way
City, Zip	Santa Clara, 95054
Telephone	(408) 980–9515
Ownership	Municipal
Weekday Fee	$12
Weekend Fee	$18
Twilight Fee	$7
Men's Par	72
Men's Yardage	6474
Men's Rating	70.3
Women's Par	72
Women's Yardage	6078
Women's Rating	73.8
Championship Yardage	6853
Championship Rating	72.1

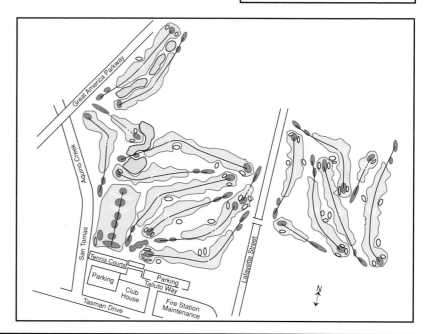

OVERALL APPEAL	Good	9	of possible	15
DESIGN & VARIETY	Good	9	of possible	15
SCENERY	Good	9	of possible	15
OVERALL DIFFICULTY	Very Good	8	of possible	10
GREENS DIFFICULTY	Very Good	8	of possible	10
OVERALL CONDITION	Very Good	8	of possible	10
GREENS CONDITION	Good	6	of possible	10
HAZARDS	Good	6	of possible	10
COSMETICS	Very Good	4	of possible	5
TOTAL	**Good**	**67**	**of possible**	**100**

Description This new course has many small hills and wide fairways that are bordered by very young trees. Many bunkers and some water provide the hazards. The back nine has panoramic views of the Silicon Valley. A lot of holes have both blind shots off the tee and approach shots to the green. Many holes tend to look the same. Management has obviously taken pride in the overall facilities and give golfers an excellent, upbeat atmosphere. 1st BEST PRACTICE FACILITIES 9th BEST CLUBHOUSE

QUALITY RANKING 38th VALUE RANKING 22nd
Clubhouse Facilities EXCELLENT Pro shop, snack bar, full bar, fine dining
Practice Facilities EXCELLENT Driving range, putting green
Who Should Play Everyone

Walkability Moderate

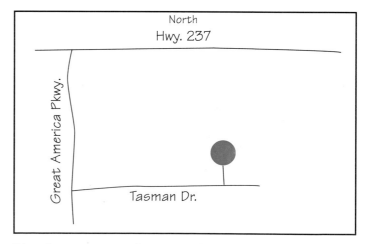

Directions *From Highway 237: Go south on Great America Parkway. Go east on Tasman Drive to the golf course.*

| Quality Rating | **29** |
| Value Rating | **D** |

FAIRWAY GLENN GOLF COURSE

Address	1661 Hogan Drive
City, Zip	Santa Clara, 95054
Telephone	(408) 988–4211
Ownership	Municipal
Weekday Fee	$9
Weekend Fee	$14
Twilight Fee	$7

Men's Par	71
Men's Yardage	6105
Men's Rating	67.0
Women's Par	72
Women's Yardage	5300
Women's Rating	68.5
Championship Yardage	—
Championship Rating	—

OVERALL APPEAL	Below Average	3	of possible	15
DESIGN & VARIETY	Average	6	of possible	15
SCENERY	Below Average	3	of possible	15
OVERALL DIFFICULTY	Average	4	of possible	10
GREENS DIFFICULTY	Average	4	of possible	10
OVERALL CONDITION	Below Average	2	of possible	10
GREENS CONDITION	Below Average	2	of possible	10
HAZARDS	Average	4	of possible	10
COSMETICS	Below Average	1	of possible	5
TOTAL	**Below Average**	**29**	**of possible**	**100**

Description   This course is surrounded on one side by older, residential housing and a levee on the Guadalupe River borders the other side. It is flat with narrow to medium-wide fairways bordered by middle-aged pine and eucalyptus trees. Small bunkers and some water provide additional hazards. It tends to play shorter than the yardage. Unfortunately, it is not much fun to play because of the maintenance.

QUALITY RANKING 101st VALUE RANKING 100th
Clubhouse Facilities   POOR   Snack bar, pro shop, full bar
Practice Facilities   GOOD   Putting green, matted driving range, 2 chipping greens, bunkers
Who Should Play   Those looking for convenience

Walkability   Easy

Directions   *From Highway 101: Exit Lafayette Street north. Go east on Hogan Drive to the golf course.*

Poor	Below Average	Average	Good	Very Good	Outstanding
☐	☐	■	☐	☐	☐

SAN JOSE MUNICIPAL GOLF COURSE

Address	1560 Oakland Road
City, Zip	San Jose, 95131
Telephone	(408) 287–5100
Ownership	Municipal
Weekday Fee	$11
Weekend Fee	$15
Twilight Fee	$7

Men's Par	72
Men's Yardage	6388
Men's Rating	70.7
Women's Par	72
Women's Yardage	5504
Women's Rating	68.5
Championship Yardage	6915
Championship Rating	72.8

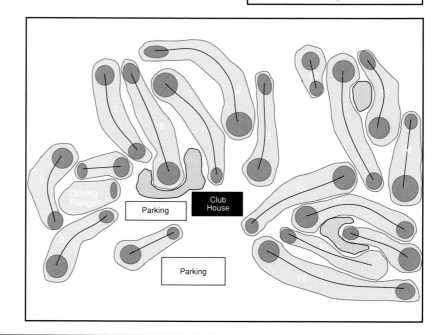

OVERALL APPEAL	Average	6	of possible	15
DESIGN & VARIETY	Average	6	of possible	15
SCENERY	Average	6	of possible	15
OVERALL DIFFICULTY	Very Good	8	of possible	10
GREENS DIFFICULTY	Good	6	of possible	10
OVERALL CONDITION	Good	6	of possible	10
GREENS CONDITION	Average	4	of possible	10
HAZARDS	Average	4	of possible	10
COSMETICS	Good	3	of possible	5
TOTAL	**Average**	**49**	**of possible**	**100**

Description This course is flat with wide fairways and bordered by young to middle-aged trees. Bunkers, some water, and long holes provide most of the hazards. There is nothing too exciting about this course nor is there anything too boring about it. A good, upbeat atmosphere is provided by the management.

QUALITY RANKING 69th   VALUE RANKING 62nd
Clubhouse Facilities   FAIR Pro shop, snack bar, full bar
Practice Facilities   GOOD Putting green, driving range, chipping green, bunker
Who Should Play Everyone

Walkability Easy

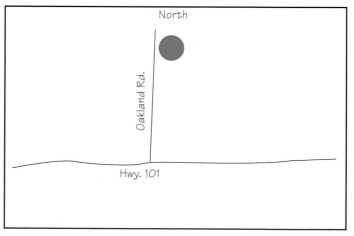

Directions *From Highway 101: Exit north on Oakland Road about 2 miles to the golf course.*

TULARCITOS GOLF AND COUNTRY CLUB

	Poor	Below Average	Average	Good	Very Good	Outstanding

TULARCITOS GOLF AND COUNTRY CLUB

Address	1200 Country Club Drive
City, Zip	Milpitas, 95035
Telephone	(408) 262–8813
Ownership	Independent
Weekday Fee	$14
Weekend Fee	$22
Twilight Fee	$7
Men's Par	72
Men's Yardage	6048
Men's Rating	69.0
Women's Par	72
Women's Yardage	5496
Women's Rating	70.3
Championship Yardage	6311
Championship Rating	70.3

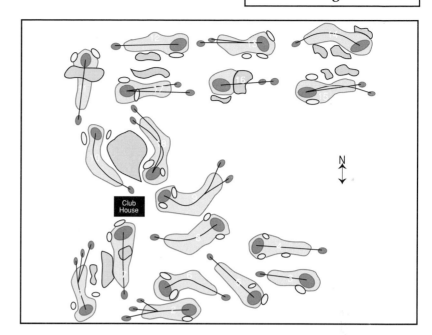

OVERALL APPEAL	Good	9	of possible	15
DESIGN & VARIETY	Good	9	of possible	15
SCENERY	Outstanding	15	of possible	15
OVERALL DIFFICULTY	Good	6	of possible	10
GREENS DIFFICULTY	Very Good	8	of possible	10
OVERALL CONDITION	Average	4	of possible	10
GREENS CONDITION	Average	4	of possible	10
HAZARDS	Good	6	of possible	10
COSMETICS	Average	2	of possible	5
TOTAL	**Good**	**63**	**of possible**	**100**

Description An extremely rugged course in the hills high above Milpitas. Narrow to wide fairways with a few young trees. Bunkers, some water, and mostly hills provide the hazards. Excellent, panoramic view of the Bay Area from the front nine while the back side winds through a separate canyon. Expensive homes dot the hillside above the course. The 10th and 18th holes surround a lake which will give some golfers a good opportunity of cutting corners.

QUALITY RANKING 43rd VALUE RANKING 34th
Clubhouse Facilities GOOD Pro shop, snack bar, full bar, coffee shop
Practice Facilities FAIR Putting green, driving range (lake)
Who Should Play Everyone

Walkability Difficult

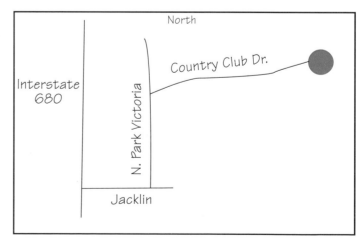

Directions *From I680: Exit east on Jacklin. Go north on N. Park Victoria. Go east on Country Club to the course.*

SPRING VALLEY GOLF COURSE

Quality Rating	**30**	
Value Rating	**F**	

SPRING VALLEY GOLF COURSE

Address	3441 E. Calaveras Boulevard
City, Zip	Milpitas, 95035
Telephone	(408) 262–1722
Ownership	County
Weekday Fee	$12
Weekend Fee	$16
Twilight Fee	$8

Men's Par	71
Men's Yardage	6185
Men's Rating	67.2
Women's Par	73
Women's Yardage	—
Women's Rating	—
Championship Yardage	—
Championship Rating	—

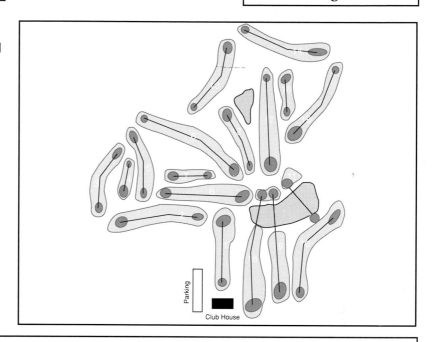

OVERALL APPEAL	Below Average	3	of possible	15
DESIGN & VARIETY	Below Average	3	of possible	15
SCENERY	Good	9	of possible	15
OVERALL DIFFICULTY	Below Average	2	of possible	10
GREENS DIFFICULTY	Average	4	of possible	10
OVERALL CONDITION	Below Average	2	of possible	10
GREENS CONDITION	Below Average	2	of possible	10
HAZARDS	Average	4	of possible	10
COSMETICS	Below Average	1	of possible	5
TOTAL	**Below Average**	**30**	**of possible**	**100**

Description   This course is flat, with a few small hills located in a valley above Milpitas. Narrow to wide fairways are bordered by young to middle-aged pine, eucalyptus, oak, and weeping willow trees. There is one lake, and little imagination in design does not allow the golfer much fun.

QUALITY RANKING   99th   VALUE RANKING 104th

Clubhouse Facilities   FAIR   Pro shop, snack bar, full bar

Practice Facilities   FAIR   Putting green, driving range

Who Should Play   Those looking for convenience

Walkability   Moderate

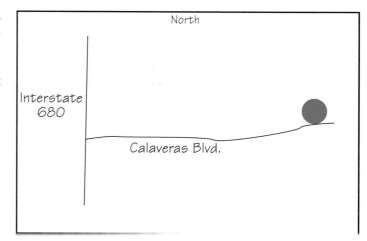

Directions   *From I680: Exit east on Calaveras Boulevard about 2 miles to the golf course.*

PLEASANT HILLS GOLF & COUNTRY CLUB

Address	2050 S. White Road
City, Zip	San Jose, 95122
Telephone	(408) 238–3485
Ownership	Independent
Weekday Fee	$11
Weekend Fee	$15
Twilight Fee	$7

Men's Par	72
Men's Yardage	6519
Men's Rating	70.0
Women's Par	75
Women's Yardage	6084
Women's Rating	—
Championship Yardage	6888
Championship Rating	—

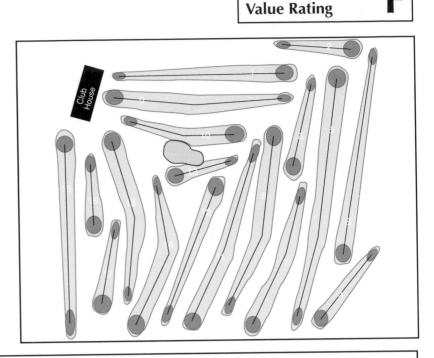

OVERALL APPEAL	Poor	0	of possible	15
DESIGN & VARIETY	Average	6	of possible	15
SCENERY	Average	6	of possible	15
OVERALL DIFFICULTY	Good	6	of possible	10
GREENS DIFFICULTY	Average	4	of possible	10
OVERALL CONDITION	Poor	0	of possible	10
GREENS CONDITION	Poor	0	of possible	10
HAZARDS	Average	4	of possible	10
COSMETICS	Poor	0	of possible	5
TOTAL	**Below Average**	**26**	**of possible**	**100**

Description This course is flat with narrow to medium-wide fairways bordered by mature pine, oak, eucalyptus, and weeping willow trees. Residential housing borders the course. It has a nice peaceful, laid-back atmosphere with beautiful trees and decent holes. However, negligent maintenance and lack of pride eliminates the fun of this course. Most holes emphasize accurate tee shots.

QUALITY RANKING 106th VALUE RANKING 106th
Clubhouse Facilities POOR Pro shop, full bar

Practice Facilities POOR Putting green

Who Should Play Those looking for convenience

Walkability Easy

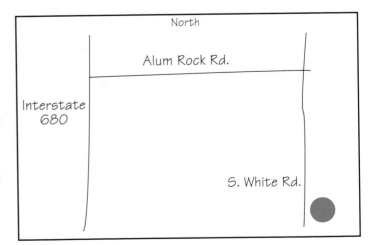

Directions *From I680: Exit east on Alum Rock Road and go about 1 mile. Go south on S. White Road about 3 miles to the course.*

Poor	Below Average	Average	Good	Very Good	Outstanding

OAK RIDGE GOLF CLUB

Address	225 Cottle Road
City, Zip	San Jose, 95123
Telephone	(408) 227–6557
Ownership	Independent
Weekday Fee	$13
Weekend Fee	$17
Twilight Fee	$9

Men's Par	72
Men's Yardage	5829
Men's Rating	67.4
Women's Par	72
Women's Yardage	5526
Women's Rating	69.8
Championship Yardage	6191
Championship Rating	69.2

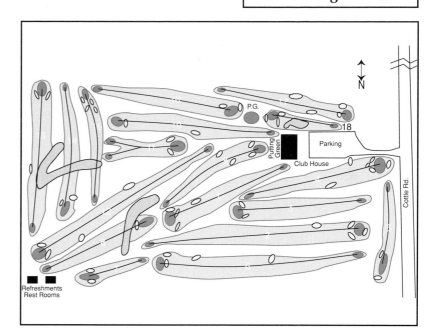

OVERALL APPEAL	Below Average	3	of possible	15
DESIGN & VARIETY	Good	9	of possible	15
SCENERY	Average	6	of possible	15
OVERALL DIFFICULTY	Average	4	of possible	10
GREENS DIFFICULTY	Average	4	of possible	10
OVERALL CONDITION	Below Average	2	of possible	10
GREENS CONDITION	Below Average	2	of possible	10
HAZARDS	Very Good	8	of possible	10
COSMETICS	Below Average	1	of possible	5
TOTAL	**Below Average**	**39**	**of possible**	**100**

Description This course is flat with lots of little mounds. It has narrow fairways bordered by middle-aged oak trees. All greens are surrounded by mature palm trees. Some very well placed water and high-lipped bunkers provide the hazards. A really nice design for a short course with some very interesting holes. You must be able to hit the ball straight. It could be a much better course with proper maintenance.

QUALITY RANKING 91st   VALUE RANKING 102nd

Clubhouse Facilities   FAIR Pro shop, snack bar, full bar, banquet

Practice Facilities   POOR 2 putting greens, chipping green

Who Should Play Everyone

Walkability Easy

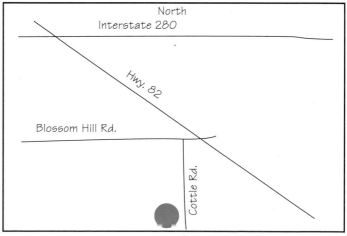

Directions *From I280: Exit south on Old Monterey Highway (Highway 82) about 4 miles. Go west on Blossom Hill Road. Go south on Cottle Road to the golf course.*

Quality Rating **73**

Value Rating **B**

SANTA TERESA GOLF CLUB

Address	260 Bernal Avenue
City, Zip	San Jose, 95119
Telephone	(408) 225–2650
Ownership	County
Weekday Fee	$14
Weekend Fee	$18
Twilight Fee	$10

Men's Par	71
Men's Yardage	6376
Men's Rating	69.9
Women's Par	73
Women's Yardage	5970
Women's Rating	72.7
Championship Yardage	6699
Championship Rating	71.4

OVERALL APPEAL	Very Good	12	of possible	15
DESIGN & VARIETY	Very Good	12	of possible	15
SCENERY	Very Good	12	of possible	15
OVERALL DIFFICULTY	Very Good	8	of possible	10
GREENS DIFFICULTY	Good	6	of possible	10
OVERALL CONDITION	Very Good	8	of possible	10
GREENS CONDITION	Good	6	of possible	10
HAZARDS	Good	6	of possible	10
COSMETICS	Good	3	of possible	5
TOTAL	**Good**	**73**	**of possible**	**100**

Description This course is flat with some rolling hills. Fairways are narrow to medium-wide bordered by young to middle-aged oak, pine, eucalyptus, and willow trees. One side of the course is surrounded by residential housing and the other side is tucked into foothills. Some water and plenty of bunkers provide the hazards. A parklike setting with a few holes having scenic views of the South Bay area. A fun and challenging course to play. Management takes pride with all facilities well maintained. 2nd BEST PRACTICE FACILITIES

QUALITY RANKING 29th   VALUE RANKING   24th
Clubhouse Facilities GOOD   Pro shop, snack bar, coffee shop
Practice Facilities EXCELLENT   Putting green, matted driving range
Who Should Play Everyone
Walkability Moderate

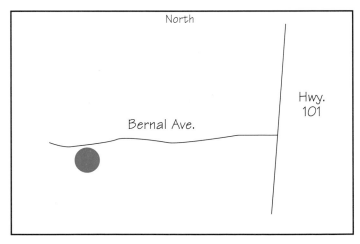

Directions   *From Highway 101: Exit west on Bernal Avenue about 1½ miles to the golf course.*

☐	☐	■	☐	☐	☐	
Poor	Below Average	Average	Good	Very Good	Outstanding	

RIVERSIDE GOLF COURSE

Address	P.O. Box 13128
City, Zip	Coyote, 95013
Telephone	(408) 463–0622
Ownership	Independent
Weekday Fee	$12
Weekend Fee	$17
Twilight Fee	$8

Men's Par	72
Men's Yardage	6504
Men's Rating	69.6
Women's Par	73
Women's Yardage	5969
Women's Rating	72.3
Championship Yardage	6825
Championship Rating	71.0

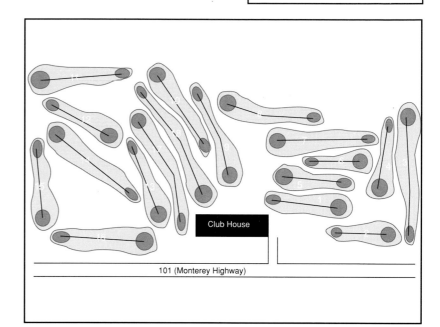

101 (Monterey Highway)

OVERALL APPEAL	Good	9	of possible	15
DESIGN & VARIETY	Average	6	of possible	15
SCENERY	Good	9	of possible	15
OVERALL DIFFICULTY	Very Good	8	of possible	10
GREENS DIFFICULTY	Good	6	of possible	10
OVERALL CONDITION	Good	6	of possible	10
GREENS CONDITION	Average	4	of possible	10
HAZARDS	Average	4	of possible	10
COSMETICS	Average	2	of possible	5
TOTAL	**Average**	**54**	**of possible**	**100**

Description This course is flat with some small hills. Wide fairways are bordered by middle-aged to mature oak and pine trees. Some holes have water hazards. There are nice views of the surrounding foothills. The front side tends to look the same with similar holes. The back side is much more interesting with a few slight doglegs.

QUALITY RANKING 52nd **VALUE RANKING 60th**

Clubhouse Facilities FAIR Pro shop, snack bar, full bar, banquet, bar-b-q area

Practice Facilities GOOD Putting green, driving range

Who Should Play Everyone

Walkability Moderate

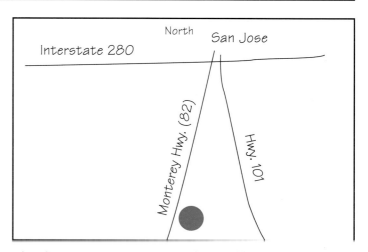

Directions *In San Jose: Go south on Old Monterey Highway (Highway 82) about 8 miles to the golf course on the left.*

| Poor | Below Average | **Average** | Good | Very Good | Outstanding |

SUNOL VALLEY GOLF CLUB— PALM

Address	6900 Mission Road
City, Zip	Sunol, 94586
Telephone	(415) 862–2404
Ownership	Independent
Weekday Fee	$20
Weekend Fee	$25
Twilight Fee	$10

Men's Par	72
Men's Yardage	6409
Men's Rating	69.5
Women's Par	74
Women's Yardage	5997
Women's Rating	73.2
Championship Yardage	6843
Championship Rating	71.7

OVERALL APPEAL	Average	6	of possible	15
DESIGN & VARIETY	Average	6	of possible	15
SCENERY	Good	9	of possible	15
OVERALL DIFFICULTY	Good	6	of possible	10
GREENS DIFFICULTY	Good	6	of possible	10
OVERALL CONDITION	Below Average	2	of possible	10
GREENS CONDITION	Below Average	2	of possible	10
HAZARDS	Below Average	2	of possible	10
COSMETICS	Average	2	of possible	5
TOTAL	**Average**	**41**	**of possible**	**100**

Description This course has rolling hills with wide fairways bordered by mostly young palm trees. Most of the course offers sweeping panoramic views of the surrounding countryside. Bunkers and some water provide the hazards. It's a wide-open course with little imagination in design. Most holes tend to look the same.

QUALITY RANKING 85th VALUE RANKING 101st
Clubhouse Facilities GOOD Pro shop, snack bar, full bar, banquet
Practice Facilities POOR Putting green

Who Should Play Everyone

Walkability Difficult (carts are mandatory on weekends)

Directions *From I680: Exit west on Andrade Road to the golf course.*

Poor	Below Average	Average	Good	Very Good	Outstanding
☐	☐	■	☐	☐	☐

Quality Rating 43

Value Rating D

SUNOL VALLEY GOLF CLUB— CYPRESS

Address	6900 Mission Road
City, Zip	Sunol, 94586
Telephone	(415) 862–2404
Ownership	Independent
Weekday Fee	$20
Weekend Fee	$25
Twilight Fee	$10

Men's Par	72
Men's Yardage	5801
Men's Rating	66.8
Women's Par	72
Women's Yardage	5458
Women's Rating	69.5
Championship Yardage	6195
Championship Rating	68.7

OVERALL APPEAL	Average	6	of possible	15
DESIGN & VARIETY	Average	6	of possible	15
SCENERY	Good	9	of possible	15
OVERALL DIFFICULTY	Average	4	of possible	10
GREENS DIFFICULTY	Good	6	of possible	10
OVERALL CONDITION	Below Average	2	of possible	10
GREENS CONDITION	Average	4	of possible	10
HAZARDS	Average	4	of possible	10
COSMETICS	Average	2	of possible	5
TOTAL	**Average**	**43**	**of possible**	**100**

Description   This course is flat with some rolling hills. Fairways are narrow to wide bordered by young to middle-aged pine trees. There are panoramic views of the surrounding foothills. It is located next to Interstate Highway 680. The front side is on top of the hill, with mostly wide fairways and very young pine trees. Most holes tend to play the same. The back side is completely different with a few interesting holes. Much larger trees are on the back side.

QUALITY RANKING   82nd   VALUE RANKING   99th
Clubhouse Facilities   GOOD   Pro shop, snack bar, full bar, banquet
Practice Facilities   POOR   Putting green

Who Should Play   Everyone

Walkability   Moderate (carts are mandatory on weekends)

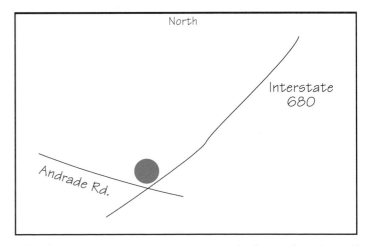

Directions   *From I680: Exit west on Andrade Road to the golf course.*

Poor	Below Average	Average	Good	Very Good	Outstanding
☐	☐	■	☐	☐	☐

Quality Rating **51**

Value Rating **C**

SKYWEST GOLF COURSE

Address	1401 Golf Course Road
City, Zip	Hayward, 94541
Telephone	(415) 278–6188
Ownership	Independent
Weekday Fee	$10
Weekend Fee	$12
Twilight Fee	—

Men's Par	72
Men's Yardage	6540
Men's Rating	69.4
Women's Par	73
Women's Yardage	6171
Women's Rating	73.9
Championship Yardage	6930
Championship Rating	71.5

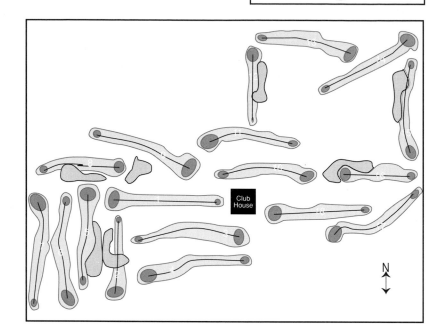

OVERALL APPEAL	Good	9	of possible	15
DESIGN & VARIETY	Average	6	of possible	15
SCENERY	Average	6	of possible	15
OVERALL DIFFICULTY	Very Good	8	of possible	10
GREENS DIFFICULTY	Good	6	of possible	10
OVERALL CONDITION	Average	4	of possible	10
GREENS CONDITION	Average	4	of possible	10
HAZARDS	Good	6	of possible	10
COSMETICS	Average	2	of possible	5
TOTAL	**Average**	**51**	**of possible**	**100**

Description This course is flat with medium-wide fairways bordered by middle-aged pine, oak, eucalyptus, and weeping willow trees. One side is bordered by Skywest Airport and the other by residential housing. The course can play very long from the championship tees. Most holes tend to play the same with the exception of a few water holes.

QUALITY RANKING 63rd VALUE RANKING 51st
Clubhouse Facilities FAIR Pro shop, snack bar, full bar
Practice Facilities FAIR Matted driving range, putting green
Who Should Play Everyone

Walkability Easy

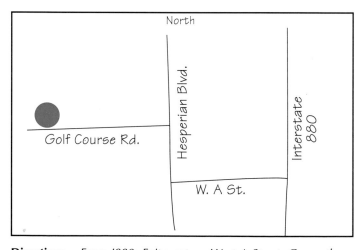

Directions *From I880: Exit west on West A Street. Go north on Hesperian Boulevard. Immediately go west on Golf Course Road to the golf course.*

Poor	Below Average	Average	Good	Very Good	Outstanding
☐	☐	■	☐	☐	☐

Quality Rating	**49**
Value Rating	**C**

SAN LEANDRO TONY LEMA GOLF COURSE

Address	13800 Neptune Drive
City, Zip	San Leandro, 94577
Telephone	(415) 895–2162
Ownership	Municipal
Weekday Fee	$8.50
Weekend Fee	$10.50
Twilight Fee	$5.50

Men's Par	71
Men's Yardage	6017
Men's Rating	67.3
Women's Par	72
Women's Yardage	5697
Women's Rating	69.6
Championship Yardage	6466
Championship Rating	71.8

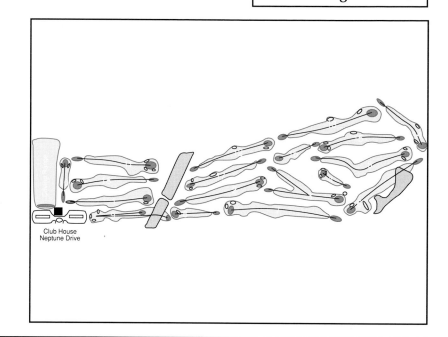

Club House
Neptune Drive

OVERALL APPEAL	Average	6	of possible	15
DESIGN & VARIETY	Average	6	of possible	15
SCENERY	Very Good	12	of possible	15
OVERALL DIFFICULTY	Good	6	of possible	10
GREENS DIFFICULTY	Good	6	of possible	10
OVERALL CONDITION	Below Average	2	of possible	10
GREENS CONDITION	Good	6	of possible	10
HAZARDS	Below Average	2	of possible	10
COSMETICS	Good	3	of possible	5
TOTAL	**Average**	**49**	**of possible**	**100**

Description This course is flat with a few small hills. Located next to San Francisco Bay it provides distant views of the San Francisco skyline. Fairways are narrow to wide with mostly very young trees. Some bunkers and water provide the hazards. Five holes are very narrow with middle-aged trees while the rest of the holes tend to be very wide and look the same. On these holes you can hit the ball almost anywhere and not get into trouble.

QUALITY RANKING 68th   VALUE RANKING 37th
Clubhouse Facilities   GOOD   Pro shop, snack bar (a new clubhouse is under construction)
Practice Facilities   GOOD   Matted and lit driving range, 2 putting greens
Who Should Play   Everyone

Walkability   Moderate

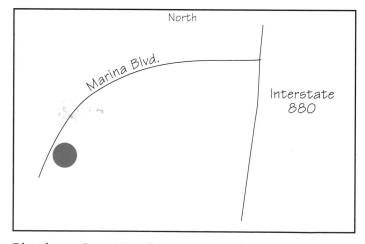

Directions   *From I880: Exit west on Marina Boulevard and go about 1½ miles to the golf course.*

Poor	Below Average	Average	Good	Very Good	Outstanding
☐	☐	☐	■	☐	☐

Quality Rating	**60**
Value Rating	**B**

LAKE CHABOT GOLF COURSE

Address	Golf Links Road
City, Zip	Oakland, 94605
Telephone	(415) 351-5812
Ownership	Municipal
Weekday Fee	$9
Weekend Fee	$12
Twilight Fee	$5

Men's Par	72
Men's Yardage	6180
Men's Rating	67.7
Women's Par	71
Women's Yardage	5362
Women's Rating	70.0
Championship Yardage	—
Championship Rating	—

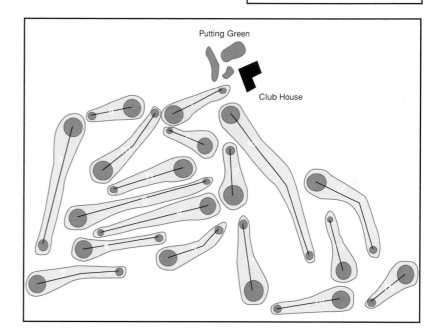

OVERALL APPEAL	Very Good	12	of possible	15
DESIGN & VARIETY	Good	9	of possible	15
SCENERY	Outstanding	15	of possible	15
OVERALL DIFFICULTY	Average	4	of possible	10
GREENS DIFFICULTY	Average	4	of possible	10
OVERALL CONDITION	Average	4	of possible	10
GREENS CONDITION	Average	4	of possible	10
HAZARDS	Good	6	of possible	10
COSMETICS	Average	2	of possible	5
TOTAL	**Good**	**60**	**of possible**	**100**

Description   This course is very hilly with narrow to wide fairways bordered by mature eucalyptus and pine trees. It has a beautiful location in the Oakland hills with some very nice views of the city below. Trees, canyons, bunkers, and hills provide the hazards. There are a lot of interesting holes and a peaceful setting makes for a very enjoyable round of golf. With better maintenance, this course could be much improved. The 18th hole is a 665 yard, par 6 hole that is straight downhill. 9th BEST SCENERY

QUALITY RANKING   46th   VALUE RANKING   11th
Clubhouse Facilities   FAIR   Pro shop, snack bar
Practice Facilities   FAIR   Matted driving range, putting green
Who Should Play   Everyone
Walkability   Difficult

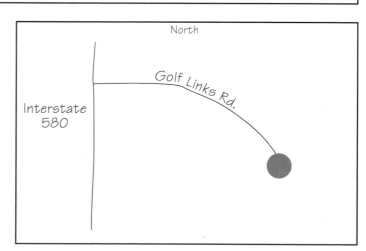

Directions   *From I580: Exit east on Golf Links Road and go about 2 miles to the golf course.*

Quality Rating	**17**
Value Rating	**F**

LEW F. GALBRAITH GOLF COURSE

Address	10505 Doolittle Drive
City, Zip	Oakland, 94603
Telephone	(415) 569–9411
Ownership	Municipal
Weekday Fee	$8
Weekend Fee	$12
Twilight Fee	$6

Men's Par	72
Men's Yardage	6298
Men's Rating	69.9
Women's Par	72
Women's Yardage	5732
Women's Rating	71.7
Championship Yardage	6777
Championship Rating	71.1

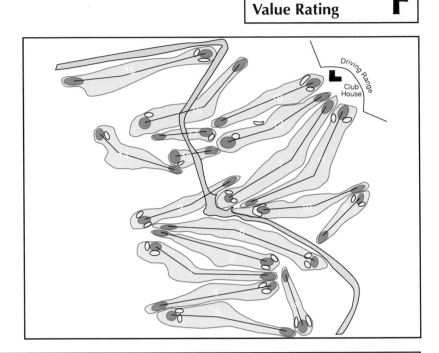

OVERALL APPEAL	Poor	0	of possible	15
DESIGN & VARIETY	Poor	0	of possible	15
SCENERY	Poor	0	of possible	15
OVERALL DIFFICULTY	Very Good	8	of possible	10
GREENS DIFFICULTY	Average	4	of possible	10
OVERALL CONDITION	Poor	0	of possible	10
GREENS CONDITION	Below Average	2	of possible	10
HAZARDS	Below Average	2	of possible	10
COSMETICS	Below Average	1	of possible	5
TOTAL	**Poor**	**17**	**of possible**	**100**

Description This course is flat with medium to wide fairways bordered by young to middle-aged trees. It is surrounded by the Oakland Airport and industrial areas. Bunkers and trees provide the hazards. This is a boring course with most holes looking the same. With negligent maintenance it's not much fun playing here.

QUALITY RANKING 110th VALUE RANKING 110th
Clubhouse Facilities FAIR Pro shop, snack bar

Practice Facilities GOOD Lit driving range, putting green, bunkers
Who Should Play Those looking for convenience

Walkability Easy

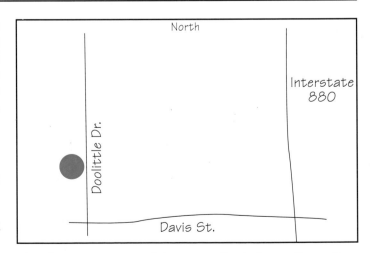

Directions *From I880: Exit west on Davis Street. Go north on Doolittle Drive to the golf course.*

Poor	Below Average	Average	Good	Very Good	Outstanding
☐	☐	■	☐	☐	☐

Quality Rating	**51**
Value Rating	**C**

WILLOW PARK GOLF COURSE

Address	17007 Redwood Road
City, Zip	Castro Valley, 94546
Telephone	(415) 537–8989
Ownership	Independent
Weekday Fee	$11
Weekend Fee	$14
Twilight Fee	—

Men's Par	71
Men's Yardage	5465
Men's Rating	67.9
Women's Par	71
Women's Yardage	5200
Women's Rating	68.5
Championship Yardage	6070
Championship Rating	—

OVERALL APPEAL	Good	9	of possible	15
DESIGN & VARIETY	Average	6	of possible	15
SCENERY	Very Good	12	of possible	15
OVERALL DIFFICULTY	Average	4	of possible	10
GREENS DIFFICULTY	Average	4	of possible	10
OVERALL CONDITION	Average	4	of possible	10
GREENS CONDITION	Average	4	of possible	10
HAZARDS	Good	6	of possible	10
COSMETICS	Average	2	of possible	5
TOTAL	**Average**	**51**	**of possible**	**100**

Description   Located in two heavily wooded canyons, this course is flat with a few small hills. Fairways are very narrow and bordered by middle-aged oak trees. A small creek runs throughout the course. Not too long and difficult, this course is pleasant to play because of its remoteness and beauty. Emphasis is on accurate driving. A small herd of deer usually roams the fairways. It's hard to tell you are near a metropolitan area.

QUALITY RANKING 65th   VALUE RANKING 58th
Clubhouse Facilities GOOD   Pro shop, snack bar, full bar, fine dining, banquet
Practice Facilities POOR   Matted driving range (lake), putting green
Who Should Play   High-handicappers or those looking for scenery
Walkability   Moderate

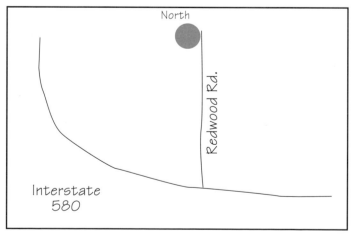

Directions   *From I580: Exit north on Redwood Road and go about 2 ½ miles to the golf course.*

ALAMEDA GOLF CLUB—JACK CLARK

Poor	Below Average	Average	Good	Very Good	Outstanding

ALAMEDA GOLF CLUB— JACK CLARK

Address	Memorial Clubhouse Road
City, Zip	Alameda, 94501
Telephone	(415) 522–4321
Ownership	Municipal
Weekday Fee	$7
Weekend Fee	$10
Twilight Fee	$6

Men's Par	71
Men's Yardage	6107
Men's Rating	67.3
Women's Par	71
Women's Yardage	5473
Women's Rating	73
Championship Yardage	6559
Championship Rating	69.4

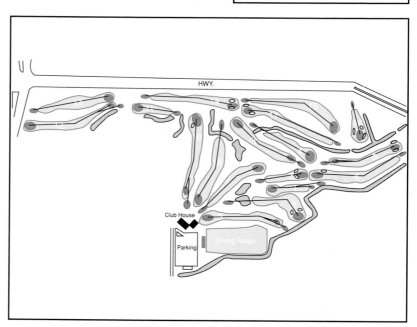

OVERALL APPEAL	Average	6	of possible	15
DESIGN & VARIETY	Average	6	of possible	15
SCENERY	Average	6	of possible	15
OVERALL DIFFICULTY	Good	6	of possible	10
GREENS DIFFICULTY	Average	4	of possible	10
OVERALL CONDITION	Below Average	2	of possible	10
GREENS CONDITION	Average	4	of possible	10
HAZARDS	Average	4	of possible	10
COSMETICS	Below Average	1	of possible	5
TOTAL	**Below Average**	**39**	**of possible**	**100**

Description This course is flat with medium to wide fairways bordered by young to middle-aged trees. The Oakland Airport is on one side and residential housing is on the other side. Some water and bunkers provide the hazards. For the most part, this course has little imagination and is not too well maintained. However, some holes have water, which makes for interesting play.

QUALITY RANKING 92nd VALUE RANKING 73rd
Clubhouse Facilities FAIR Pro shop, snack bar, full bar
Practice Facilities FAIR Matted driving range, 2 putting greens
Who Should Play Those looking for convenience

Walkability Easy

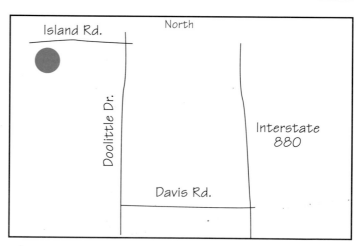

Directions *From I880: Exit west on Davis Road about 1½ miles. Go north on Doolittle for about 2 miles. Go west on Island Road to the golf course.*

ALAMEDA GOLF CLUB—EARL FRY

| Poor | Below Average | Average | Good | Very Good | Outstanding |

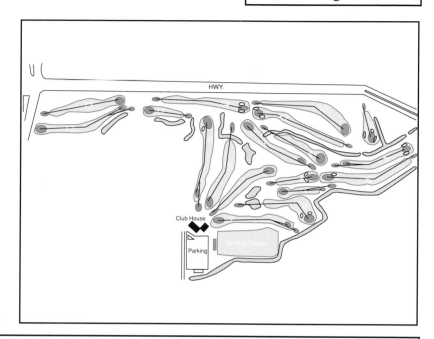

Quality Rating 53

Value Rating B

ALAMEDA GOLF CLUB— EARL FRY

Address	Memorial Clubhouse Road
City, Zip	Alameda, 94501
Telephone	(415) 522–4321
Ownership	Municipal
Weekday Fee	$7
Weekend Fee	$10
Twilight Fee	$6

Men's Par	71
Men's Yardage	5826
Men's Rating	66.4
Women's Par	71
Women's Yardage	5505
Women's Rating	70.2
Championship Yardage	6141
Championship Rating	68.4

OVERALL APPEAL	Good	9	of possible	15
DESIGN & VARIETY	Good	9	of possible	15
SCENERY	Average	6	of possible	15
OVERALL DIFFICULTY	Average	4	of possible	10
GREENS DIFFICULTY	Good	6	of possible	10
OVERALL CONDITION	Good	6	of possible	10
GREENS CONDITION	Good	6	of possible	10
HAZARDS	Good	6	of possible	10
COSMETICS	Below Average	1	of possible	5
TOTAL	**Average**	**53**	**of possible**	**100**

Description This course is flat with narrow to medium-wide fairways bordered by mature pine, oak, and eucalyptus trees. Lots of water and bunkers provide additional hazards. It's located next to the Oakland International Airport. This is a fun course to play that's not too difficult and with interesting holes. The par 5's are rather short. Water definitely comes into play on many holes.

QUALITY RANKING 58th VALUE RANKING 19th

Clubhouse Facilities FAIR Pro shop, snack bar, full bar

Practice Facilities FAIR Matted driving range, 2 putting greens

Who Should Play Everyone

Walkability Easy

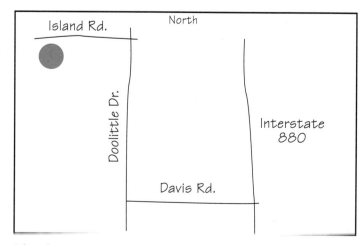

Directions *From I880: Exit west on Davis Road about 1½ miles. Go north on Doolittle for about 2 miles. Go west on Island Road to the golf course.*

53

☐	☐	■	☐	☐	☐
Poor	Below Average	Average	Good	Very Good	Outstanding

LAS POSITAS GOLF COURSE

Address	909 Clubhouse Drive
City, Zip	Livermore, 94550
Telephone	(415) 443–3122
Ownership	Municipal
Weekday Fee	$10
Weekend Fee	$14
Twilight Fee	$7
Men's Par	72
Men's Yardage	6466
Men's Rating	70.8
Women's Par	73
Women's Yardage	5697
Women's Rating	71.2
Championship Yardage	6740
Championship Rating	—

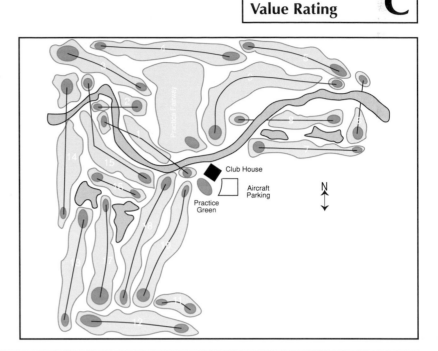

OVERALL APPEAL	Average	6	of possible	15
DESIGN & VARIETY	Good	9	of possible	15
SCENERY	Average	6	of possible	15
OVERALL DIFFICULTY	Good	6	of possible	10
GREENS DIFFICULTY	Average	4	of possible	10
OVERALL CONDITION	Below Average	2	of possible	10
GREENS CONDITION	Average	4	of possible	10
HAZARDS	Good	6	of possible	10
COSMETICS	Average	2	of possible	5
TOTAL	**Average**	**45**	**of possible**	**100**

Description This course is mostly flat with some rolling hills. Narrow to wide fairways are bordered by young to middle-aged trees. The Livermore Airport is on one side while Interstate 580 is on the other side. There is some water. The front side has some interesting holes with much larger trees. The back side is flat and a little bit more boring.

QUALITY RANKING 79th VALUE RANKING 61st
Clubhouse Facilities GOOD Pro shop, snack bar, full bar, fine dining
Practice Facilities GOOD Driving range, putting green
Who Should Play Everyone

Walkability Moderate

54

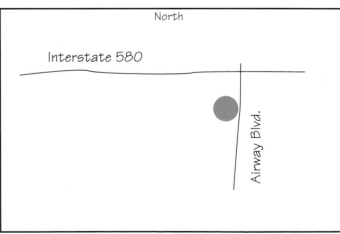

Directions *From I580: Exit south on Airway Boulevard to the golf course.*

	Poor	Below Average	Average	Good	Very Good	Outstanding

CANYON LAKES COUNTRY CLUB

Address	Country Club Drive
City, Zip	San Ramon, 94583
Telephone	(415) 867–0600
Ownership	Independent
Weekday Fee	$25
Weekend Fee	$30
Twilight Fee	—

Men's Par	71
Men's Yardage	5975
Men's Rating	68.5
Women's Par	71
Women's Yardage	5234
Women's Rating	—
Championship Yardage	6379
Championship Rating	70.4

OVERALL APPEAL	Outstanding	15	of possible	15
DESIGN & VARIETY	Outstanding	15	of possible	15
SCENERY	Outstanding	15	of possible	15
OVERALL DIFFICULTY	Very Good	8	of possible	10
GREENS DIFFICULTY	Outstanding	10	of possible	10
OVERALL CONDITION	Outstanding	10	of possible	10
GREENS CONDITION	Outstanding	10	of possible	10
HAZARDS	Outstanding	10	of possible	10
COSMETICS	Outstanding	5	of possible	5
TOTAL	**Outstanding**	**98**	**of possible**	**100**

Description This course is hilly with medium to wide fairways bordered by very young trees. It weaves throughout a close-gated community of upscale housing. Canyons, lakes, and beautiful bunkers are the hazards. Located in the foothills, some holes offer excellent views of the valley below. Exceptionally well designed and challenging for all golfers. 3rd BEST OVERALL CONDITION 4th BEST GREENS CONDITION 4th BEST "FUN COURSE" 6th BEST COSMETICS 9th BEST DESIGN

QUALITY RANKING **4th** **VALUE RANKING** **18th**
Clubhouse Facilities **FAIR** Pro shop (temporary)

Practice Facilities **POOR** Putting green (temporary)

Who Should Play Everyone
Walkability Moderate (carts are mandatory and must stay on paths)

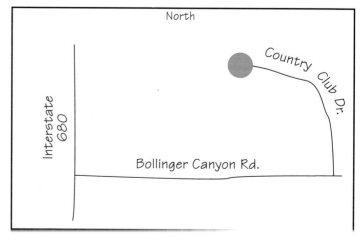

Directions *From I680: Exit east on Bollinger Canyon Road about 2½ miles. Go north on Country Club Drive to the golf course.*

SAN RAMON ROYAL VISTA GOLF CLUB

☐	☐	■	☐	☐	☐
Poor	Below Average	Average	Good	Very Good	Outstanding

SAN RAMON ROYAL VISTA GOLF CLUB

Address	9430 Fircrest Lane
City, Zip	San Ramon, 94583
Telephone	(415) 828–6100
Ownership	Independent
Weekday Fee	$12
Weekend Fee	$18
Twilight Fee	$7.50

Men's Par	72
Men's Yardage	6300
Men's Rating	69.3
Women's Par	73
Women's Yardage	5814
Women's Rating	72.0
Championship Yardage	6538
Championship Rating	70.5

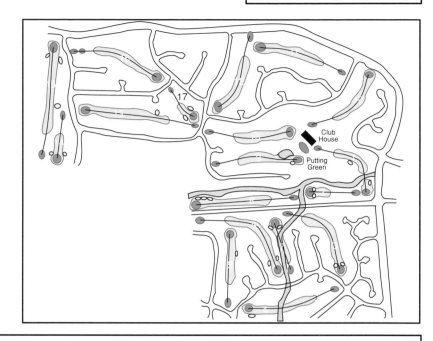

OVERALL APPEAL	Average	6	of possible	15
DESIGN & VARIETY	Average	6	of possible	15
SCENERY	Average	6	of possible	15
OVERALL DIFFICULTY	Good	6	of possible	10
GREENS DIFFICULTY	Average	4	of possible	10
OVERALL CONDITION	Average	4	of possible	10
GREENS CONDITION	Average	4	of possible	10
HAZARDS	Average	4	of possible	10
COSMETICS	Below Average	1	of possible	5
TOTAL	**Average**	**41**	**of possible**	**100**

Description   This course is flat with a few small hills and gullies. It weaves through a residential area with medium to wide fairways bordered by young to mature pine and oak trees. Bunkers and some water provide additional hazards. A few interesting holes and a few boring holes make this course quite average. The back side is more interesting than the front side.

QUALITY RANKING 86th   VALUE RANKING   76th
Clubhouse Facilities   GOOD Pro shop, coffee shop, full bar, banquet
Practice Facilities   FAIR   Driving range, putting green

Who Should Play Everyone

Walkability Moderate

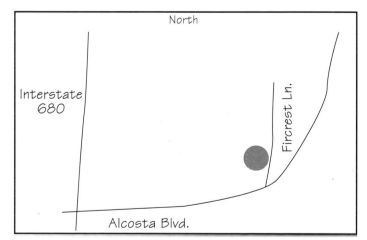

Directions   *From I680: Exit east on Alcosta Boulevard. Go north on Fircrest Lane to the golf course.*

BOUNDARY OAK GOLF COURSE

Address	3800 Valley Vista Road
City, Zip	Walnut Creek, 94598
Telephone	(415) 934–6211
Ownership	Municipal
Weekday Fee	$10
Weekend Fee	$14
Twilight Fee	$5

Men's Par	72
Men's Yardage	6406
Men's Rating	70.2
Women's Par	72
Women's Yardage	5699
Women's Rating	72.0
Championship Yardage	6788
Championship Rating	72.0

OVERALL APPEAL	Very Good	12	of possible	15
DESIGN & VARIETY	Outstanding	15	of possible	15
SCENERY	Outstanding	15	of possible	15
OVERALL DIFFICULTY	Very Good	8	of possible	10
GREENS DIFFICULTY	Very Good	8	of possible	10
OVERALL CONDITION	Good	6	of possible	10
GREENS CONDITION	Average	4	of possible	10
HAZARDS	Very Good	8	of possible	10
COSMETICS	Average	2	of possible	5
TOTAL	**Good**	**78**	**of possible**	**100**

Description This course has rolling hills with medium-wide fairways bordered by a variety of middle-aged trees. Located in the foothills it has excellent views of the valley below. Trees, some water, and many well-placed bunkers provide the hazards. This course should be fun for all levels of players. With more attention to maintenance, it could be a premier municipal course.

QUALITY RANKING 22nd VALUE RANKING 4th
Clubhouse Facilities GOOD Pro shop, snack bar, full bar, fine dining, banquets
Practice Facilities GOOD Lit driving range, 2 putting greens, bunker
Who Should Play Everyone

Walkability Moderate

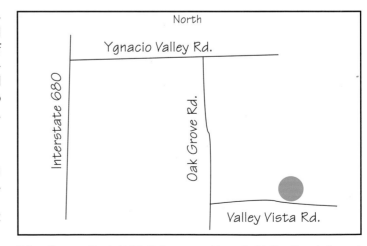

Directions *From I680: Exit east on Ygnacio Valley Road about 4 miles. Go south on Oak Grove Road. Go east on Valley Vista Road to the golf course.*

Poor	Below Average	Average	Good	Very Good	Outstanding

DIABLO CREEK GOLF COURSE

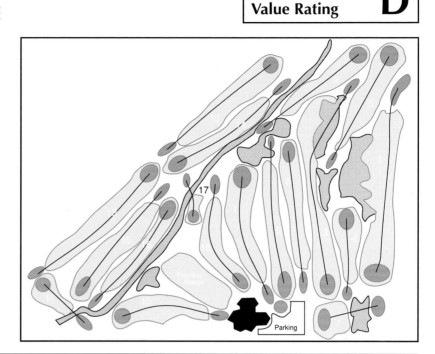

Address	4050 Port Chicago Way
City, Zip	Concord, 94520
Telephone	(415) 686–6262
Ownership	Municipal
Weekday Fee	$9
Weekend Fee	$11
Twilight Fee	$5.50

Men's Par	72
Men's Yardage	6324
Men's Rating	69.5
Women's Par	72
Women's Yardage	5962
Women's Rating	73.1
Championship Yardage	—
Championship Rating	—

OVERALL APPEAL	Below Average	3	of possible	15
DESIGN & VARIETY	Below Average	3	of possible	15
SCENERY	Below Average	3	of possible	15
OVERALL DIFFICULTY	Average	4	of possible	10
GREENS DIFFICULTY	Average	4	of possible	10
OVERALL CONDITION	Average	4	of possible	10
GREENS CONDITION	Average	4	of possible	10
HAZARDS	Average	4	of possible	10
COSMETICS	Below Average	1	of possible	5
TOTAL	**Below Average**	**30**	**of possible**	**100**

Description This course is flat with narrow to wide fairways bordered by young to middle-aged trees. Highway 4 is on one side and the other side has industrial buildings. Bunkers and water are most of the hazards. Little imagination in design, poor scenery, and average maintenance make for a poor round of golf.

QUALITY RANKING 100th   VALUE RANKING   97th
Clubhouse Facilities   FAIR Pro shop, snack bar, full bar
Practice Facilities   FAIR Matted driving range, putting green
Who Should Play Those looking for convenience

Walkability Easy

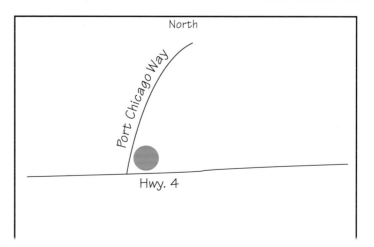

Directions *From Highway 4: Exit north on Port Chicago Way to the golf course.*

Quality Rating	**19**	
Value Rating	**F**	

LONE TREE GOLF COURSE

Address	Route 1, Box 1200, Lone Tree Way
City, Zip	Antioch, 94509
Telephone	(415) 757–5200
Ownership	Municipal
Weekday Fee	$6.50
Weekend Fee	$9
Twilight Fee	—

Men's Par	73
Men's Yardage	5970
Men's Rating	67.1
Women's Par	74
Women's Yardage	5615
Women's Rating	72.1
Championship Yardage	6298
Championship Rating	68.8

OVERALL APPEAL	Poor	0	of possible	15
DESIGN & VARIETY	Below Average	3	of possible	15
SCENERY	Average	6	of possible	15
OVERALL DIFFICULTY	Below Average	2	of possible	10
GREENS DIFFICULTY	Below Average	2	of possible	10
OVERALL CONDITION	Poor	0	of possible	10
GREENS CONDITION	Average	4	of possible	10
HAZARDS	Below Average	2	of possible	10
COSMETICS	Poor	0	of possible	5
TOTAL	**Poor**	**19**	**of possible**	**100**

Description   This course is hilly with medium to wide fairways bordered by young to middle-aged trees. It is located in the foothills above Antioch. Bunkers provide most of the hazards. The management doesn't show much pride in maintaining this course. There are plenty of elevated tee boxes and elevated greens. The back side is better designed than the front side.

QUALITY RANKING 109th   VALUE RANKING 109th
Clubhouse Facilities   FAIR   Pro shop, snack bar, full bar, banquet
Practice Facilities   FAIR   Driving range, putting green

Who Should Play   Those looking for convenience

Walkability   Moderate

North

Hwy. 4

Lone Tree Way

Directions   *From Highway 4: Exit south on Lone Tree Way for about 2 miles to the golf course.*

Poor	Below Average	Average	Good	Very Good	Outstanding
☐	☐	■	☐	☐	☐

Quality Rating	**54**
Value Rating	**B**

BLUE ROCK SPRINGS MUNICIPAL GOLF COURSE

Address	P.O. Box 4069
City, Zip	Vallejo, 94590
Telephone	(707) 643–8476
Ownership	Municipal
Weekday Fee	$8
Weekend Fee	$11
Twilight Fee	$4

Men's Par	72
Men's Yardage	6152
Men's Rating	68.2
Women's Par	73
Women's Yardage	5879
Women's Rating	72.9
Championship Yardage	—
Championship Rating	—

OVERALL APPEAL	Good	9	of possible	15
DESIGN & VARIETY	Good	9	of possible	15
SCENERY	Good	9	of possible	15
OVERALL DIFFICULTY	Average	4	of possible	10
GREENS DIFFICULTY	Good	6	of possible	10
OVERALL CONDITION	Average	4	of possible	10
GREENS CONDITION	Good	6	of possible	10
HAZARDS	Average	4	of possible	10
COSMETICS	Good	3	of possible	5
TOTAL	**Average**	**54**	**of possible**	**100**

Description   This course has both flat and hilly holes with wide fairways bordered by middle-aged pine and weeping willow trees. It is located in the foothills with distant views of residential housing. Sand traps provide most of the hazards. Some of the holes are very interesting while others tend to be average.

QUALITY RANKING   55th   **VALUE RANKING**   28th
Clubhouse Facilities   **FAIR**   Pro shop, snack bar, banquet
Practice Facilities   **POOR**   Putting green, chipping green, bunker
Who Should Play   Everyone

Walkability   Moderate

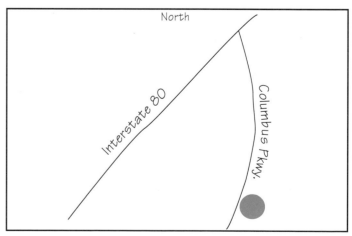

Directions   *From I80: Exit south on Columbus Parkway about 5 miles to the golf course.*

FRANKLIN CANYON GOLF COURSE

Quality Rating	**75**
Value Rating	**B**

FRANKLIN CANYON GOLF COURSE

Address	Highway 4
City, Zip	Rodeo, 94572
Telephone	(415) 799–6191
Ownership	Independent
Weekday Fee	$12
Weekend Fee	$18
Twilight Fee	$7

Men's Par	72
Men's Yardage	6202
Men's Rating	69.3
Women's Par	72
Women's Yardage	5516
Women's Rating	70.9
Championship Yardage	6776
Championship Rating	71.3

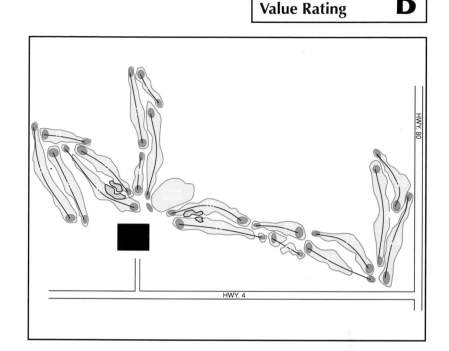

OVERALL APPEAL	Very Good	12	of possible	15
DESIGN & VARIETY	Outstanding	15	of possible	15
SCENERY	Good	9	of possible	15
OVERALL DIFFICULTY	Very Good	8	of possible	10
GREENS DIFFICULTY	Very Good	8	of possible	10
OVERALL CONDITION	Good	6	of possible	10
GREENS CONDITION	Good	6	of possible	10
HAZARDS	Very Good	8	of possible	10
COSMETICS	Good	3	of possible	5
TOTAL	**Good**	**75**	**of possible**	**100**

Description This course is flat with a few hills, located in a canyon alongside Highway 4. Medium to wide fairways are bordered by young to middle-aged oak and pine trees. Plenty of bunkers, lakes, and ravines also provide hazards. An exciting design and good maintenance make golf very enjoyable at this course. There are many "gambler's" holes for those golfers who like to cut corners.

QUALITY RANKING 27th   VALUE RANKING 17th

Clubhouse Facilities   FAIR   Pro shop, Snack bar, full bar

Practice Facilities   FAIR   Matted driving range, 2 putting greens

Who Should Play   Everyone

Walkability   Moderate

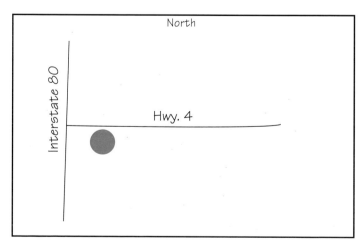

Directions   *From I80: Go east on Highway 4 about 3 miles to the golf course.*

TILDEN PARK GOLF COURSE

Quality Rating **64**

Value Rating **A**

TILDEN PARK GOLF COURSE

Address	Grizzly Peak and Shasta roads
City, Zip	Berkeley, 94708
Telephone	(415) 848–7373
Ownership	Independent
Weekday Fee	$9
Weekend Fee	$12
Twilight Fee	$6

Men's Par	70
Men's Yardage	5823
Men's Rating	67.5
Women's Par	71
Women's Yardage	5399
Women's Rating	69.9
Championship Yardage	6294
Championship Rating	69.5

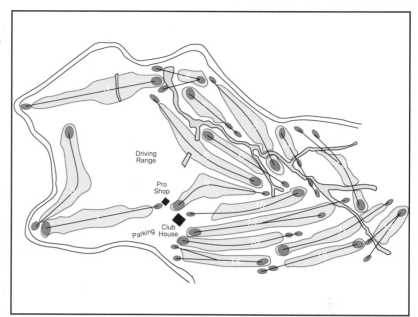

OVERALL APPEAL	Very Good	12	of possible	15
DESIGN & VARIETY	Very Good	12	of possible	15
SCENERY	Outstanding	15	of possible	15
OVERALL DIFFICULTY	Good	6	of possible	10
GREENS DIFFICULTY	Good	6	of possible	10
OVERALL CONDITION	Average	4	of possible	10
GREENS CONDITION	Below Average	2	of possible	10
HAZARDS	Good	6	of possible	10
COSMETICS	Below Average	1	of possible	5
TOTAL	**Good**	**64**	**of possible**	**100**

Description This course is hilly with narrow to wide fairways bordered by magnificent, mature eucalyptus and pine trees. It is located high up in the Berkeley hills in Tilden Regional Park. Some bunkers, ravines, and hills provide additional hazards. There are lots of interesting holes with either elevated tee boxes or elevated greens. A beautiful and remote setting makes it hard to believe a few million people are just around the corner. With better maintenance, it could be an outstanding course to play.

QUALITY RANKING 40th   VALUE RANKING   7th
Clubhouse Facilities   FAIR   Pro shop, snack bar

Practice Facilities   FAIR   Matted driving range, putting green, chipping area, bunker
Who Should Play   Everyone

Walkability   Difficult

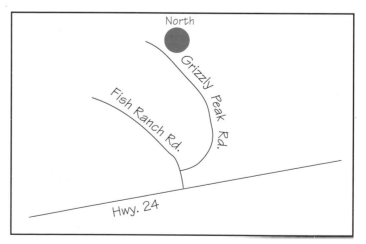

Directions   *From Highway 24: Exit north on Fish Ranch Road. Go north on Grizzly Peak Road to the golf course.*

Poor	Below Average	Average	Good	Very Good	Outstanding
☐	☐	☐	☐	☐	■

Quality Rating	**94**
Value Rating	**C**

CHARDONNAY CLUB

Address	2555 Jameson Canyon Road
City, Zip	Napa, 94558
Telephone	(707) 257–8950
Ownership	Independent
Weekday Fee	$30
Weekend Fee	$30
Twilight Fee	$10

Men's Par	72
Men's Yardage	6235
Men's Rating	69.4
Women's Par	72
Women's Yardage	5388
Women's Rating	70.9
Championship Yardage	7087
Championship Rating	73.1

OVERALL APPEAL	Outstanding	15	of possible	15
DESIGN & VARIETY	Outstanding	15	of possible	15
SCENERY	Outstanding	15	of possible	15
OVERALL DIFFICULTY	Outstanding	10	of possible	10
GREENS DIFFICULTY	Outstanding	10	of possible	10
OVERALL CONDITION	Very Good	8	of possible	10
GREENS CONDITION	Very Good	8	of possible	10
HAZARDS	Outstanding	10	of possible	10
COSMETICS	Good	3	of possible	5
TOTAL	**Outstanding**	**94**	**of possible**	**100**

Description   This course is hilly with wide fairways and only a few trees scattered around. It is located in rolling foothills with excellent panoramic views. Large, contoured bunkers, waste bunkers, high grass, ravines, creeks, and lakes provide excellent hazards. It is a world-class golf course with every hole very exciting to play. It has a Scottish flavor with many landing areas surrounded by numerous hazards. 2nd BEST DESIGN 3rd BEST "FUN COURSE" 4th BEST HAZARDS 5th BEST FINISHING HOLE 6th MOST DIFFICULT GREENS 8th MOST DIFFICULT COURSE 10th BEST GREENS CONDITION

QUALITY RANKING   7th   VALUE RANKING   57th
Clubhouse Facilities   GOOD   Pro shop (temporary)
Practice Facilities   GOOD   Driving range, putting
  green
Who Should Play   Everyone
Walkability   Carts are mandatory

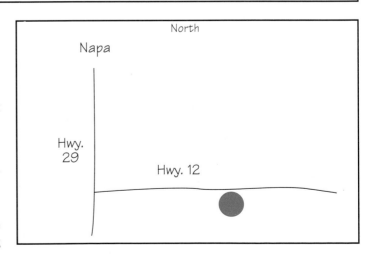

Directions   *From Napa: Go south on Highway 29 about 3 miles. Go east on Highway 12 about 3 miles to the golf course.*

Poor	Below Average	Average	Good	Very Good	Outstanding
☐	☐	■	☐	☐	☐

Quality Rating **45**

Value Rating **C**

SONOMA NATIONAL GOLF CLUB

Address	17700 Arnold Drive
City, Zip	Sonoma, 95416
Telephone	(707) 996–0300
Ownership	Independent
Weekday Fee	$11
Weekend Fee	$16
Twilight Fee	$10

Men's Par	72
Men's Yardage	6391
Men's Rating	70.9
Women's Par	74
Women's Yardage	5937
Women's Rating	73.3
Championship Yardage	6672
Championship Rating	72.0

OVERALL APPEAL	Average	6	of possible	15
DESIGN & VARIETY	Good	9	of possible	15
SCENERY	Good	9	of possible	15
OVERALL DIFFICULTY	Good	6	of possible	10
GREENS DIFFICULTY	Average	4	of possible	10
OVERALL CONDITION	Below Average	2	of possible	10
GREENS CONDITION	Average	4	of possible	10
HAZARDS	Average	4	of possible	10
COSMETICS	Below Average	1	of possible	5
TOTAL	**Average**	**45**	**of possible**	**100**

Description This course has rolling hills with medium-wide fairways bordered by middle-aged eucalyptus, pine, and oak trees. It's located near Sonoma in the Valley of the Moon. Bunkers and trees provide the hazards. With this peaceful setting and a decent design, this course can be fun to play. It could be a much better golf course with proper maintenance.

QUALITY RANKING **77th** **VALUE RANKING** **67th**
Clubhouse Facilities **FAIR** Pro shop, coffee shop, full bar, banquet
Practice Facilities **POOR** Putting green, bunker

Who Should Play Everyone

Walkability Moderate

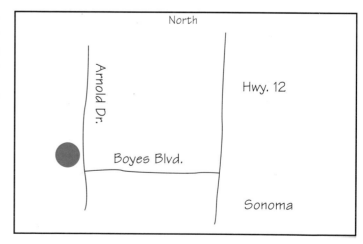

Directions *From Highway 12: Go west on Boyes Boulevard. Go north on Arnold Drive to the Golf Course.*

NAPA MUNICIPAL GOLF COURSE—KENNEDY PARK

	Poor	Below Average	Average	Good	Very Good	Outstanding

Good (marked)

Quality Rating 73

Value Rating A

NAPA MUNICIPAL GOLF COURSE—KENNEDY PARK

Address	2295 Streblow Drive
City, Zip	Napa, 94558
Telephone	(707) 255–4333
Ownership	Municipal
Weekday Fee	$9
Weekend Fee	$12
Twilight Fee	$5.50

Men's Par	72
Men's Yardage	6480
Men's Rating	70.2
Women's Par	73
Women's Yardage	5920
Women's Rating	73.6
Championship Yardage	6713
Championship Rating	71.5

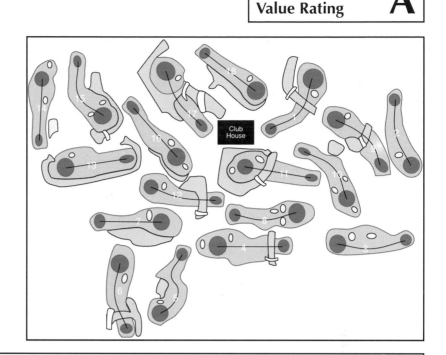

OVERALL APPEAL	Very Good	12	of possible	15
DESIGN & VARIETY	Outstanding	15	of possible	15
SCENERY	Good	9	of possible	15
OVERALL DIFFICULTY	Outstanding	10	of possible	10
GREENS DIFFICULTY	Good	6	of possible	10
OVERALL CONDITION	Average	4	of possible	10
GREENS CONDITION	Good	6	of possible	10
HAZARDS	Outstanding	10	of possible	10
COSMETICS	Below Average	1	of possible	5
TOTAL	**Good**	**73**	**of possible**	**100**

Description This course is flat to hilly with narrow to wide fairways bordered by middle-aged oak and pine trees. It is located in the Napa Valley with many water hazards, trees, and bunkers. It's a very challenging course with a wide variety of golf holes. With more attention to maintenance and cosmetics, it could be an outstanding golf course.

QUALITY RANKING 30th   VALUE RANKING 3rd
Clubhouse Facilities FAIR Pro shop, snack bar, full bar
Practice Facilities FAIR Driving range, putting green

Who Should Play Everyone

Walkability Moderate

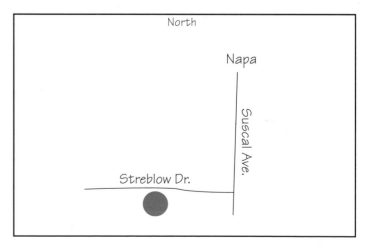

Directions *From downtown Napa: Go south on Suscol Avenue about 2 miles. Go west on Streblow Drive to the golf course.*

Poor	Below Average	Average	Good	Very Good	Outstanding
☐	☐	☐	☐	■	☐

Quality Rating **88**

Value Rating **A**

OAKMONT GOLF COURSE —WEST

Address	7025 Oakmont Drive
City, Zip	Santa Rosa, 95405
Telephone	(707) 539–0415
Ownership	Independent
Weekday Fee	$15
Weekend Fee	$17
Twilight Fee	$9

Men's Par	72
Men's Yardage	6048
Men's Rating	68.7
Women's Par	72
Women's Yardage	5506
Women's Rating	70.7
Championship Yardage	6417
Championship Rating	70.6

OVERALL APPEAL	Outstanding	15	of possible	15
DESIGN & VARIETY	Outstanding	15	of possible	15
SCENERY	Very Good	12	of possible	15
OVERALL DIFFICULTY	Very Good	8	of possible	10
GREENS DIFFICULTY	Very Good	8	of possible	10
OVERALL CONDITION	Good	6	of possible	10
GREENS CONDITION	Outstanding	10	of possible	10
HAZARDS	Outstanding	10	of possible	10
COSMETICS	Very Good	4	of possible	5
TOTAL	**Very Good**	**88**	**of possible**	**100**

Description This course is flat with medium to wide fairways bordered by mature pine, oak, and other trees. It weaves throughout an upscale retirement community that is very well manicured. Numerous water hazards and well-placed bunkers provide the hazards. It has excellent design for all levels of golfers. It's located in the Valley of the Moon. Also, the surrounding homes have beautiful landscaping, giving additional beauty to the golf course. 3rd BEST GREENS CONDITION 7th BEST PRACTICE FACILITIES 8th BEST CLUBHOUSE

QUALITY RANKING 12th VALUE RANKING 5th
Clubhouse Facilities EXCELLENT Pro shop, snack bar, full bar, fine dining
Practice Facilities EXCELLENT Driving range, putting green
Who Should Play Everyone

Walkability Easy

70

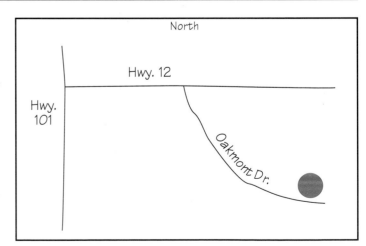

Directions *From Highway 101: Exit east on Highway 12 for about 8 miles. Go south on Oakmont Drive to the golf course.*

| Poor | Below Average | Average | Good | Very Good | Outstanding |

Quality Rating 53

Value Rating B

BENNETT VALLEY GOLF COURSE

Address	3330 Yulupa Avenue
City, Zip	Santa Rosa, 95405
Telephone	(707) 528–3673
Ownership	Municipal
Weekday Fee	$7
Weekend Fee	$10
Twilight Fee	$4.50

Men's Par	71
Men's Yardage	6107
Men's Rating	68.5
Women's Par	73
Women's Yardage	5808
Women's Rating	71.6
Championship Yardage	6484
Championship Rating	70.0

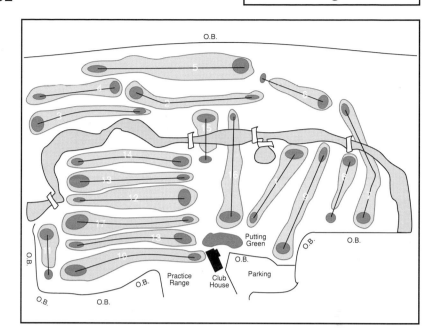

OVERALL APPEAL	Good	9	of possible	15
DESIGN & VARIETY	Good	9	of possible	15
SCENERY	Good	9	of possible	15
OVERALL DIFFICULTY	Good	6	of possible	10
GREENS DIFFICULTY	Average	4	of possible	10
OVERALL CONDITION	Below Average	2	of possible	10
GREENS CONDITION	Good	6	of possible	10
HAZARDS	Good	6	of possible	10
COSMETICS	Average	2	of possible	5
TOTAL	**Average**	**53**	**of possible**	**100**

Description This course is flat with a few small hills. Fairways are narrow to medium-wide and are bordered by mature pine, eucalyptus, and oak trees. The course is surrounded by residential housing. Trees, bunkers, and some water provide the hazards. The front side has many interesting holes which are fun to play. The back side tends to be boring with most holes playing the same. With better maintenance, it could be a good golf course.

QUALITY RANKING 57th VALUE RANKING 20th
Clubhouse Facilities FAIR Pro shop, snack bar, full bar
Practice Facilities FAIR Driving range, putting green

Who Should Play Everyone

Walkability Easy

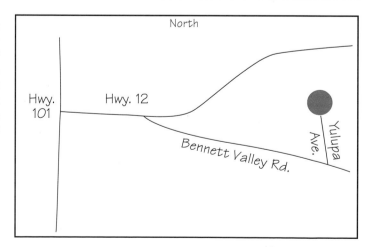

Directions *From Highway 101: Exit east on Highway 12 about 1 mile. Go east on Bennett Valley Road to Yulupa Avenue and the golf course.*

FOUNTAINGROVE COUNTRY CLUB

Poor	Below Average	Average	Good	Very Good	Outstanding
☐	☐	☐	☐	☐	■

FOUNTAINGROVE COUNTRY CLUB

Address	1525 Fountaingrove Parkway
City, Zip	Santa Rosa, 95401
Telephone	(707) 579–4653
Ownership	Independent
Weekday Fee	$22
Weekend Fee	$45
Twilight Fee	$6

Men's Par	72
Men's Yardage	6380
Men's Rating	70.9
Women's Par	72
Women's Yardage	5644
Women's Rating	72.6
Championship Yardage	6797
Championship Rating	72.9

OVERALL APPEAL	Outstanding	15	of possible	15
DESIGN & VARIETY	Outstanding	15	of possible	15
SCENERY	Outstanding	15	of possible	15
OVERALL DIFFICULTY	Outstanding	10	of possible	10
GREENS DIFFICULTY	Outstanding	10	of possible	10
OVERALL CONDITION	Very Good	8	of possible	10
GREENS CONDITION	Very Good	8	of possible	10
HAZARDS	Outstanding	10	of possible	10
COSMETICS	Outstanding	5	of possible	5
TOTAL	**Outstanding**	**96**	**of possible**	**100**

Description   This course is hilly with narrow to wide fairways bordered by mature oak trees. Located in the foothills east of Santa Rosa, it has a very peaceful atmosphere as it winds through the rugged hills. There are lakes, streams, and plenty of contoured bunkers. It has an exciting design which is both challenging and pleasurable to play—top–notch all the way. 1st BEST COSMETICS 3rd BEST CLUBHOUSE 7th MOST DIFFICULT GREENS 8th BEST HAZARDS 8th BEST DESIGN 9th MOST DIFFICULT 10th BEST PRACTICE FACILITIES

QUALITY RANKING   5th   VALUE RANKING   13th
Clubhouse Facilities   EXCELLENT   Pro shop, full bar, fine dining, banquet
Practice Facilities   GOOD   Driving range, 2 putting greens
Who Should Play   Everyone
Walkability   Moderate (carts are mandatory and must stay on paths)

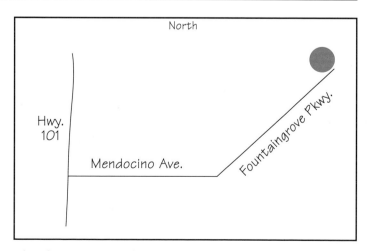

Directions   *From Highway 101: Exit east on Mendocino Avenue. Go up the hill on Fountaingrove Parkway to the course.*

| Poor | Below Average | Average | Good | Very Good | Outstanding |

Quality Rating **54**

Value Rating **C**

MOUNTAIN SHADOWS GOLF COURSE—NORTH

Address	100 Golf Course Drive
City, Zip	Rohnert Park, 94928
Telephone	(707) 584–7766
Ownership	Municipal
Weekday Fee	$10
Weekend Fee	$15
Twilight Fee	$6

Men's Par	72
Men's Yardage	6160
Men's Rating	67.5
Women's Par	72
Women's Yardage	5503
Women's Rating	70.4
Championship Yardage	7035
Championship Rating	72.1

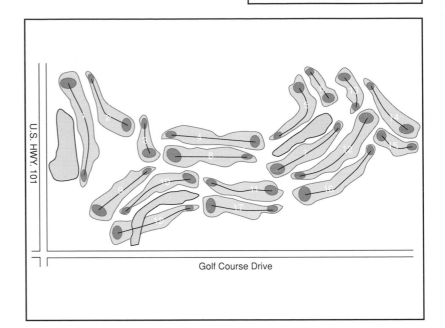

Golf Course Drive

OVERALL APPEAL	Good	9	of possible	15
DESIGN & VARIETY	Average	6	of possible	15
SCENERY	Good	9	of possible	15
OVERALL DIFFICULTY	Very Good	8	of possible	10
GREENS DIFFICULTY	Good	6	of possible	10
OVERALL CONDITION	Good	6	of possible	10
GREENS CONDITION	Average	4	of possible	10
HAZARDS	Average	4	of possible	10
COSMETICS	Average	2	of possible	5
TOTAL	**Average**	**54**	**of possible**	**100**

Description This course is flat with very wide fairways bordered by young pine trees. It weaves through residential housing with distant views of the Santa Rosa Mountains. Plenty of bunkers and water provide additional hazards. Many of the holes tend to look the same. It would be a much nicer course if the lakes would have water in them. 9th BEST FINISHING HOLE

QUALITY RANKING 53rd VALUE RANKING 45th
Clubhouse Facilities FAIR Pro shop, snack bar, full bar
Practice Facilities FAIR Driving range, putting green

Who Should Play Everyone

Walkability Easy (carts mandatory after 10 A.M.)

North

Hwy. 101

Golf Course Dr.

Directions *From Highway 101: Exit east on Golf Course Drive about ½ mile to the golf course.*

| Poor | Below Average | Average | Good | Very Good | Outstanding |

MOUNTAIN SHADOWS GOLF COURSE—SOUTH

Address	100 Golf Course Drive
City, Zip	Rohnert Park, 94928
Telephone	(707) 584–7766
Ownership	Municipal
Weekday Fee	$8
Weekend Fee	$12
Twilight Fee	$6

Men's Par	72
Men's Yardage	6500
Men's Rating	69.7
Women's Par	72
Women's Yardage	5806
Women's Rating	71.8
Championship Yardage	—
Championship Rating	—

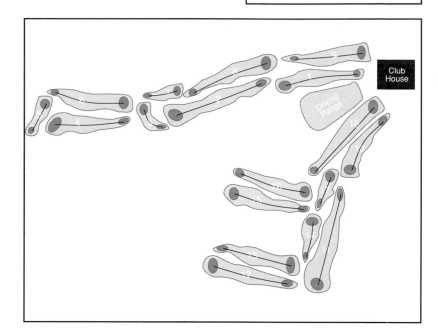

OVERALL APPEAL	Average	6	of possible	15
DESIGN & VARIETY	Average	6	of possible	15
SCENERY	Good	9	of possible	15
OVERALL DIFFICULTY	Average	4	of possible	10
GREENS DIFFICULTY	Average	4	of possible	10
OVERALL CONDITION	Average	4	of possible	10
GREENS CONDITION	Average	4	of possible	10
HAZARDS	Average	4	of possible	10
COSMETICS	Average	2	of possible	5
TOTAL	**Average**	**43**	**of possible**	**100**

Description This course is flat with medium-wide fairways bordered by young to middle-aged trees. One side has railroad tracks and the other side is surrounded by residential housing. Some bunkers and water provide the hazards. Almost all the holes are rather straight and they tend to look the same. This course is a good example of an average golf course.

QUALITY RANKING 83rd   VALUE RANKING 46th
Clubhouse Facilities   FAIR Pro shop, snack bar, full bar
Practice Facilities   FAIR Driving range, putting green

Who Should Play Everyone

Walkability Easy

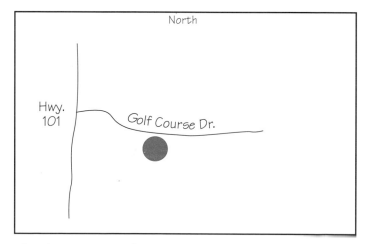

Directions *From Highway 101: Exit east on Golf Course Drive about ½ mile to the golf course.*

Quality Rating	**85**
Value Rating	**C**

BODEGA HARBOUR GOLF LINKS

Address	21301 Heron Drive
City, Zip	Bodega Bay, 94923
Telephone	(707) 875–3538
Ownership	Independent
Weekday Fee	$26
Weekend Fee	$31
Twilight Fee	—

Men's Par	70
Men's Yardage	5630
Men's Rating	69.1
Women's Par	70
Women's Yardage	4746
Women's Rating	65.1
Championship Yardage	6220
Championship Rating	71.8

OVERALL APPEAL	Very Good	12	of possible	15
DESIGN & VARIETY	Very Good	12	of possible	15
SCENERY	Outstanding	15	of possible	15
OVERALL DIFFICULTY	Outstanding	10	of possible	10
GREENS DIFFICULTY	Outstanding	10	of possible	10
OVERALL CONDITION	Good	6	of possible	10
GREENS CONDITION	Good	6	of possible	10
HAZARDS	Outstanding	10	of possible	10
COSMETICS	Very Good	4	of possible	5
TOTAL	**Very Good**	**85**	**of possible**	**100**

Description   This course's front side is completely different from the back side. The front side is extremely difficult with a Scottish design. It has huge mounds, deep sand and pot bunkers, and almost no trees. It is very hilly with medium-wide fairways. The back side is more traditional with some very interesting and fun holes. The course weaves throughout a residential area consisting of beautiful, natural-looking homes. There are nice distant views of Bodega Harbour. 4th BEST FINISHING HOLE 6th BEST HAZARDS 9th MOST DIFFICULT GREENS 10th BEST SCENERY

QUALITY RANKING   14th   VALUE RANKING   43rd
Clubhouse Facilities   GOOD   Pro shop, snack bar, full bar, fine dining
Practice Facilities   POOR   Putting green

Who Should Play   Everyone

Walkability   Difficult

Directions   Go south on Highway 1 about 1 mile. Go west on South Harbor. Go right on Heron Drive to the golf course.

Quality Rating	**32**
Value Rating	**F**

PEACOCK GAP GOLF & COUNTRY CLUB

Address	333 Biscayne Drive
City, Zip	San Rafael, 94901
Telephone	(415) 453-4940
Ownership	Independent
Weekday Fee	$20
Weekend Fee	$25
Twilight Fee	$13

Men's Par	71
Men's Yardage	5928
Men's Rating	67.4
Women's Par	72
Women's Yardage	5540
Women's Rating	71.4
Championship Yardage	6284
Championship Rating	69.7

OVERALL APPEAL	Below Average	3	of possible	15
DESIGN & VARIETY	Below Average	3	of possible	15
SCENERY	Good	9	of possible	15
OVERALL DIFFICULTY	Average	4	of possible	10
GREENS DIFFICULTY	Below Average	2	of possible	10
OVERALL CONDITION	Below Average	2	of possible	10
GREENS CONDITION	Average	4	of possible	10
HAZARDS	Average	4	of possible	10
COSMETICS	Below Average	1	of possible	5
TOTAL	**Below Average**	**32**	**of possible**	**100**

Description This course is flat with a few small hills. Fairways are bordered by a variety of middle-aged trees. The course is surrounded by residential housing. Bunkers, trees, and some water provide the hazards. Most of the holes aren't too well designed and are boring to play.

QUALITY RANKING 97th VALUE RANKING 108th
Clubhouse Facilities GOOD Pro shop, full bar, coffee shop, banquet
Practice Facilities FAIR Driving range, putting green

Who Should Play Those looking for convenience

Walkability Moderate

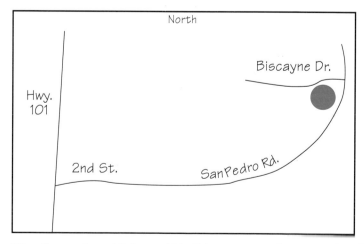

Directions *From Highway 101: Exit east on 2nd Street and go east on San Pedro Road about 4 miles to the golf course.*

INDIAN VALLEY GOLF CLUB

Poor	Below Average	Average	Good	Very Good	Outstanding
☐	☐	☐	■	☐	☐

Quality Rating 61

Value Rating C

INDIAN VALLEY GOLF CLUB

Address	P.O. Box 351
City, Zip	Novato, 94948
Telephone	(415) 897–1118
Ownership	Independent
Weekday Fee	$15
Weekend Fee	$20
Twilight Fee	$10

Men's Par	72
Men's Yardage	6120
Men's Rating	69.2
Women's Par	72
Women's Yardage	5363
Women's Rating	69.9
Championship Yardage	6272
Championship Rating	—

OVERALL APPEAL	Good	9	of possible	15
DESIGN & VARIETY	Very Good	12	of possible	15
SCENERY	Very Good	12	of possible	15
OVERALL DIFFICULTY	Good	6	of possible	10
GREENS DIFFICULTY	Good	6	of possible	10
OVERALL CONDITION	Average	4	of possible	10
GREENS CONDITION	Average	4	of possible	10
HAZARDS	Good	6	of possible	10
COSMETICS	Average	2	of possible	5
TOTAL	**Good**	**61**	**of possible**	**100**

Description This course is very hilly with medium to wide fairways bordered by middle-aged oak and pine trees. It's located in the countryside with lots of elevated tee boxes and nice, scenic views. Bunkers and hills are most of the hazards. Because of its interesting design and location, golfers can have an enjoyable time at this course.

QUALITY RANKING 45th   VALUE RANKING 44th
Clubhouse Facilities   FAIR   Pro shop, snack bar, full bar
Practice Facilities   FAIR   Driving range, putting green

Who Should Play   Everyone

Walkability   Difficult

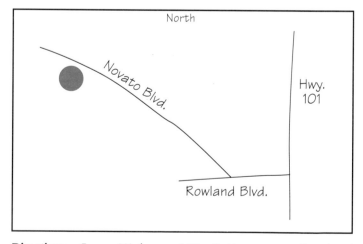

Directions   *From Highway 101: Exit west on Rowland Boulevard. Go west on Novato about 4 miles to the golf course.*

79

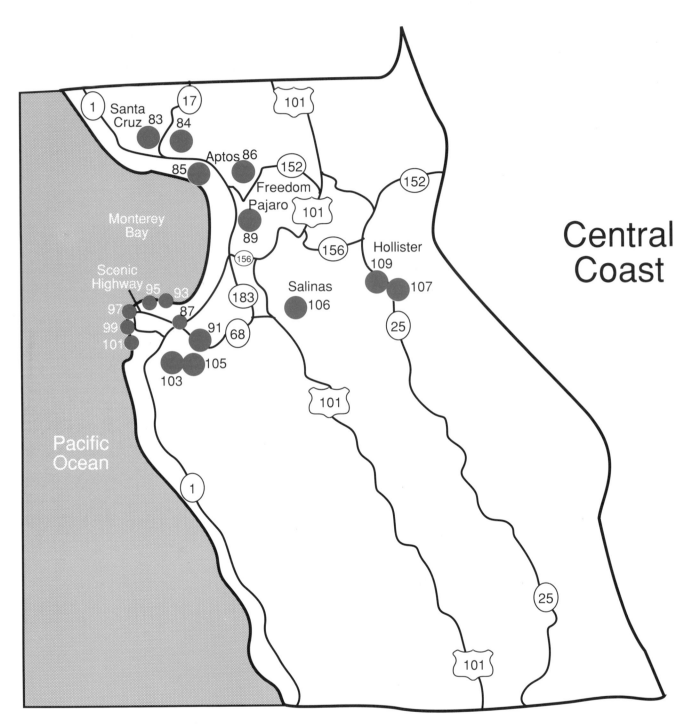

Central Coast

Numbered dots indicate the page number where the golf course is described.

CENTRAL COAST

The Central Coast zone is a golfers' paradise. It covers an area from the Pacific Ocean in the west to Hollister in the east, and from Santa Cruz in the north to the Monterey Peninsula in the south. Most of the golf courses are located in Santa Cruz or the Monterey Peninsula. They dominate Northern California when it comes to the best courses. With spectacular scenery and well-designed courses, this area offers the most to the player seeking high-quality golf.

Weather conditions in this zone can change dramatically. You can have fog in the mornings and beautiful, sunny conditions in the afternoon. Wind can come up in the afternoon, making playing conditions much more difficult. Overall, moderate weather provides plenty of good golfing days each year. Just come prepared with short-sleeved shirts, sweaters, and maybe a windbreaker jacket.

Municipal/county golf courses are very limited in this area. They are moderately priced and many people play them. Be sure to get a tee time prior to playing. A relaxed atmosphere tends to be the rule.

Independent golf courses are expensive in this area. Usually, they are maintained better than average. The atmosphere at most of them is quite formal. They also get lots of play. It is wise to make tee times ahead, especially if you plan playing in the mornings or the weekend.

You will find the ultimate in golf resorts in this area. They are upscale and formal and some are "world-class." They're expensive, but usually offer golf packages to help reduce costs. Definitely bring your formal golf attire to these courses.

Poor	Below Average	Average	Good	Very Good	Outstanding
☐	☐	☐	☐	☐	■

Quality Rating	**94**
Value Rating	**C**

PASATIEMPO GOLF CLUB

Address	18 Clubhouse Road
City, Zip	Santa Cruz, 95061
Telephone	(408) 426-3622
Ownership	Independent
Weekday Fee	$45
Weekend Fee	$55
Twilight Fee	$22.50

Men's Par	71
Men's Yardage	6154
Men's Rating	70.9
Women's Par	72
Women's Yardage	5647
Women's Rating	72.6
Championship Yardage	6483
Championship Rating	72.3

OVERALL APPEAL	Outstanding	15	of possible	15
DESIGN & VARIETY	Outstanding	15	of possible	15
SCENERY	Outstanding	15	of possible	15
OVERALL DIFFICULTY	Outstanding	10	of possible	10
GREENS DIFFICULTY	Outstanding	10	of possible	10
OVERALL CONDITION	Very Good	8	of possible	10
GREENS CONDITION	Good	6	of possible	10
HAZARDS	Outstanding	10	of possible	10
COSMETICS	Outstanding	5	of possible	5
TOTAL	**Outstanding**	**94**	**of possible**	**100**

Description   This course has rolling hills with narrow to medium-wide fairways bordered by beautiful, mature pine, oak, and eucalyptus trees. It is surrounded by residential housing with distant views of the Pacific Ocean. Many excellent bunkers, wooded ravines, and trees provide the hazards. It's a classic golf course with an excellent selection of holes. 4th BEST PRACTICE FACILITIES 5th BEST DESIGN 5th BEST HAZARDS 5th BEST COSMETICS 6th BEST "FUN COURSE" 8th MOST DIFFICULT GREENS 8th BEST CONDITION

QUALITY RANKING   6th   VALUE RANKING   66th
Clubhouse Facilities   GOOD Pro shop, snack bar, full bar, fine dining
Practice Facilities   EXCELLENT Driving range, putting green, chipping green, bunkers
Who Should Play   Everyone

Walkability   Moderate

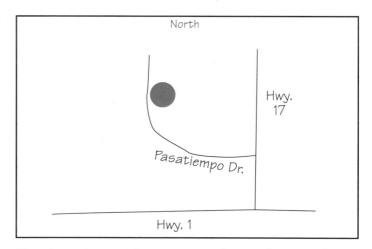

Directions   *From Highway 1: Go north on Highway 17 about 1 mile. Exit west on Pasatiempo Drive to the golf course.*

	Quality Rating	**82**
	Value Rating	**B**

DE LAVEAGA GOLF COURSE

Address	De Laveaga Park Drive
City, Zip	Santa Cruz, 95055
Telephone	(408) 423–7212
Ownership	Municipal
Weekday Fee	$15.75
Weekend Fee	$21
Twilight Fee	$10.50

Men's Par	71
Men's Yardage	5658
Men's Rating	68.2
Women's Par	71
Women's Yardage	5067
Women's Rating	70.4
Championship Yardage	—
Championship Rating	—

OVERALL APPEAL	Outstanding	15	of possible	15
DESIGN & VARIETY	Outstanding	15	of possible	15
SCENERY	Outstanding	15	of possible	15
OVERALL DIFFICULTY	Very Good	8	of possible	10
GREENS DIFFICULTY	Good	6	of possible	10
OVERALL CONDITION	Good	6	of possible	10
GREENS CONDITION	Good	6	of possible	10
HAZARDS	Very Good	8	of possible	10
COSMETICS	Good	3	of possible	5
TOTAL	**Very Good**	**82**	**of possible**	**100**

Description   This course has rolling hills with narrow to medium-wide fairways bordered by mature pine and eucalyptus trees. It is located in the hills above Santa Cruz in De Laveaga Park. Beautiful trees, canyons, bunkers, and a lake provide the hazards. It's very challenging with some extremely narrow fairways. It's also very fun to play with some very good golf holes.

QUALITY RANKING   16th   VALUE RANKING   14th
Clubhouse Facilities   GOOD   Pro shop, snack bar, coffee shop
Practice Facilities   POOR   Driving range, putting green
Who Should Play   Everyone

Walkability   Moderate

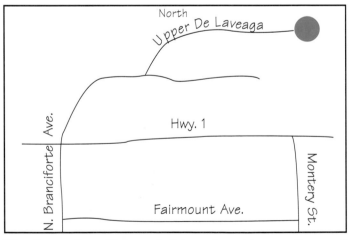

Directions   *From Highway 1: Exit south on Monterey Street and immediately go west on Fairmount Avenue. Go north and up the hill on N. Branciforte. Go north on Upper De Laveaga to the golf course.*

Quality Rating	**81**
Value Rating	**B**

APTOS SEASCAPE GOLF COURSE

Address	610 Clubhouse Drive
City, Zip	Aptos, 95003
Telephone	(408) 688–3213
Ownership	Independent
Weekday Fee	$20
Weekend Fee	$30
Twilight Fee	$15

Men's Par	72
Men's Yardage	6054
Men's Rating	69.0
Women's Par	72
Women's Yardage	5656
Women's Rating	71.7
Championship Yardage	—
Championship Rating	—

OVERALL APPEAL	Outstanding	15	of possible	15
DESIGN & VARIETY	Outstanding	15	of possible	15
SCENERY	Outstanding	15	of possible	15
OVERALL DIFFICULTY	Good	6	of possible	10
GREENS DIFFICULTY	Good	6	of possible	10
OVERALL CONDITION	Good	6	of possible	10
GREENS CONDITION	Good	6	of possible	10
HAZARDS	Very Good	8	of possible	10
COSMETICS	Very Good	4	of possible	5
TOTAL	**Very Good**	**81**	**of possible**	**100**

Description This course has rolling hills with narrow to wide fairways bordered by beautiful, mature pine and eucalyptus trees. It weaves through residential housing. Trees, bunkers, and out-of-bounds provide the hazards. It is a very enjoyable course to play. The design allows for challenging play, yet it doesn't punish you. This course is in a beautiful location and is very green and lush. 1st BEST "FUN COURSE" 6th BEST CLUBHOUSE

QUALITY RANKING 18th VALUE RANKING 21st
Clubhouse Facilities EXCELLENT Pro shop, snack bar, full bar, fine dining, banquet
Practice Facilities POOR Driving range, 2 putting greens
Who Should Play Everyone

Walkability Moderate

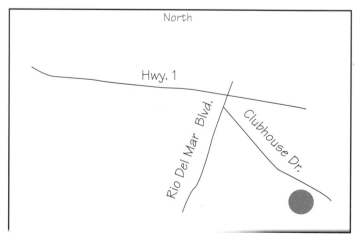

Directions *From Highway 1: Exit west on Rio Del Mar Boulevard. Immediately go south (up the hill) on Clubhouse Drive to the golf course.*

Poor	Below Average	Average	Good	Very Good	Outstanding
☐	☐	■	☐	☐	☐

Quality Rating 47

Value Rating C

SPRING HILLS GOLF CLUB

Address	31 Smith Road
City, Zip	Watsonville, 95076
Telephone	(408) 724–1404
Ownership	Independent
Weekday Fee	$10
Weekend Fee	$13
Twilight Fee	$6

Men's Par	71
Men's Yardage	6218
Men's Rating	68.7
Women's Par	71
Women's Yardage	5428
Women's Rating	71.1
Championship Yardage	—
Championship Rating	—

OVERALL APPEAL	Average	6	of possible	15
DESIGN & VARIETY	Good	9	of possible	15
SCENERY	Very Good	12	of possible	15
OVERALL DIFFICULTY	Average	4	of possible	10
GREENS DIFFICULTY	Average	4	of possible	10
OVERALL CONDITION	Below Average	2	of possible	10
GREENS CONDITION	Good	6	of possible	10
HAZARDS	Average	4	of possible	10
COSMETICS	Poor	0	of possible	5
TOTAL	**Average**	**47**	**of possible**	**100**

Description   This course is hilly with narrow to medium-wide fairways bordered by mature oak, pine, and eucalyptus trees. It is located in the coastal foothills with nice panoramic views. Trees, bunkers, and hills provide most of the hazards. There is some water. It's a fun course to play with many interesting doglegs. There are some elevated tee boxes and some holes wind through the hills. It could be a much better course with proper maintenance.

QUALITY RANKING   71st   VALUE RANKING   56th
Clubhouse Facilities   POOR   Pro shop, snack bar

Practice Facilities   FAIR   Driving range, putting green

Who Should Play   Everyone

Walkability   Difficult

Directions   *From Highway 1: Exit east on Airport Boulevard. Go north on Green Valley Road about 3 miles. Go north on Casserly Road about 1 mile. Go north on Smith Road to the golf course.*

86

Poor	Below Average	Average	Good	Very Good	Outstanding
□	□	■	□	□	□

Quality Rating	43
Value Rating	F

DEL MONTE GOLF COURSE

Address	1300 Sylvan Road
City, Zip	Monterey, 93940
Telephone	(408) 373-2436
Ownership	Resort
Weekday Fee	$26
Weekend Fee	$28
Twilight Fee	—

Men's Par	72
Men's Yardage	6007
Men's Rating	68.7
Women's Par	74
Women's Yardage	5431
Women's Rating	70.3
Championship Yardage	6278
Championship Rating	70.0

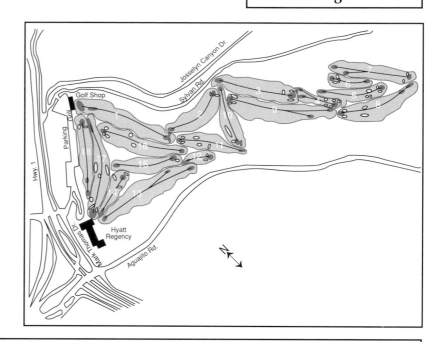

OVERALL APPEAL	Average	6	of possible	15
DESIGN & VARIETY	Average	6	of possible	15
SCENERY	Good	9	of possible	15
OVERALL DIFFICULTY	Good	6	of possible	10
GREENS DIFFICULTY	Below Average	2	of possible	10
OVERALL CONDITION	Average	4	of possible	10
GREENS CONDITION	Average	4	of possible	10
HAZARDS	Average	4	of possible	10
COSMETICS	Average	2	of possible	5
TOTAL	**Average**	**43**	**of possible**	**100**

Description This course is flat with a few small hills. It is surrounded by residential housing and the Hyatt Regency Lodge. The fairways are narrow to wide with young to middle-aged oak and pine trees. Bunkers provide additional hazards. The course has very small greens and some of the holes are rather short. Some of the holes are also boring to play. 1st BEST SCORECARD

QUALITY RANKING 81st VALUE RANKING 105th
Clubhouse Facilities FAIR Pro shop, coffee shop, full bar
Practice Facilities POOR Putting green

Who Should Play Everyone

Walkability Moderate

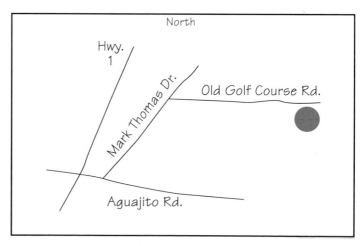

Directions *From Highway 1: Exit east on Aguajito Road (Monterey exit). Go north on Mark Thomas Drive. Go east on Old Golf Course Road to the golf course.*

PAJARO VALLEY GOLF CLUB

☐	☐	☐	■	☐	☐
Poor	Below Average	Average	Good	Very Good	Outstanding

PAJARO VALLEY GOLF CLUB

Address	967 Salinas Road
City, Zip	Watsonville, 95076
Telephone	(408) 724–3851
Ownership	Independent
Weekday Fee	$27
Weekend Fee	$30
Twilight Fee	$15

Men's Par	72
Men's Yardage	6303
Men's Rating	70.2
Women's Par	72
Women's Yardage	5642
Women's Rating	71.0
Championship Yardage	—
Championship Rating	—

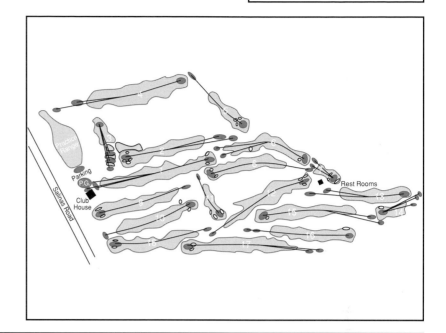

OVERALL APPEAL	Outstanding	15	of possible	15
DESIGN & VARIETY	Outstanding	15	of possible	15
SCENERY	Outstanding	15	of possible	15
OVERALL DIFFICULTY	Good	6	of possible	10
GREENS DIFFICULTY	Good	6	of possible	10
OVERALL CONDITION	Good	6	of possible	10
GREENS CONDITION	Very Good	8	of possible	10
HAZARDS	Average	4	of possible	10
COSMETICS	Average	2	of possible	5
TOTAL	**Good**	**77**	**of possible**	**100**

Description This course has rolling hills with medium to wide fairways bordered by mature pine and eucalyptus trees. It has beautiful, panoramic views of the surrounding foothills. Some bunkers, water, and trees provide the hazards. It is a fun course to play with a good selection of golf holes. There are many, elevated tee boxes. Fairways tend to be quite generous. 9th BEST "FUN COURSE"

QUALITY RANKING 23rd   VALUE RANKING   71st
Clubhouse Facilities   FAIR Pro shop, coffee shop, full bar
Practice Facilities   FAIR Driving range, 2 putting greens
Who Should Play Everyone

Walkability Difficult

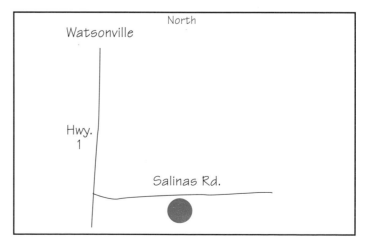

Directions Go south on Highway 1 about 3 miles. Go east on Salinas Road about 1 mile to the golf course.

LAGUNA SECA GOLF CLUB

Poor	Below Average	Average	Good	Very Good	Outstanding
☐	☐	☐	■	☐	☐

Quality Rating	**75**
Value Rating	**C**

LAGUNA SECA GOLF CLUB

Address	York Road
City, Zip	Monterey, 93940
Telephone	(408) 373–3701
Ownership	Independent
Weekday Fee	$27
Weekend Fee	$30
Twilight Fee	$15

Men's Par	71
Men's Yardage	5758
Men's Rating	67.3
Women's Par	72
Women's Yardage	5186
Women's Rating	69.4
Championship Yardage	6162
Championship Rating	69.4

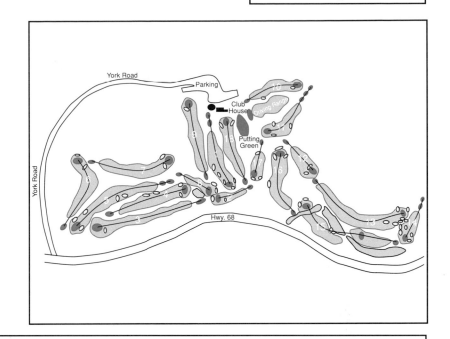

OVERALL APPEAL	Outstanding	15	of possible	15
DESIGN & VARIETY	Outstanding	15	of possible	15
SCENERY	Very Good	12	of possible	15
OVERALL DIFFICULTY	Good	6	of possible	10
GREENS DIFFICULTY	Good	6	of possible	10
OVERALL CONDITION	Average	4	of possible	10
GREENS CONDITION	Good	6	of possible	10
HAZARDS	Very Good	8	of possible	10
COSMETICS	Good	3	of possible	5
TOTAL	**Good**	**75**	**of possible**	**100**

Description   This course is hilly with narrow to medium-wide fairways bordered by mature oak trees. It is located in a rugged canyon with a few homes scattered around in the surrounding hills. There are plenty of trees, beautiful bunkers, and lakes that provide the hazards. It is a fun, short course with an excellent design. Lots of elevated tee boxes gives you some nice views.

QUALITY RANKING   26th   VALUE RANKING   74th
Clubhouse Facilities   FAIR   Pro shop, snack bar, full bar
Practice Facilities   FAIR   Putting green

Who Should Play   Everyone

Walkability   Difficult

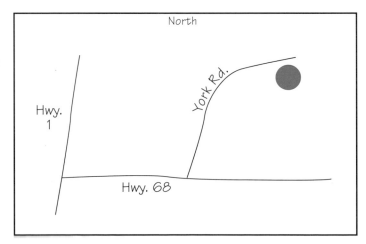

Directions   *From Highway 1: Exit east on Highway 68 for about 4 miles. Go north on York Road to the golf course.*

PACIFIC GROVE MUNICIPAL GOLF COURSE

PACIFIC GROVE MUNICIPAL GOLF COURSE

Address	77 Asilomar Boulevard
City, Zip	Pacific Grove, 93950
Telephone	(408) 375–3456
Ownership	Municipal
Weekday Fee	$12
Weekend Fee	$14
Twilight Fee	$7

Men's Par	70
Men's Yardage	5553
Men's Rating	66.3
Women's Par	72
Women's Yardage	5324
Women's Rating	70.4
Championship Yardage	—
Championship Rating	—

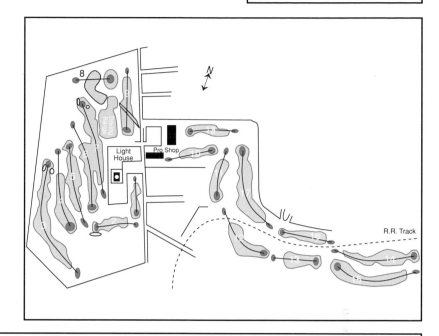

OVERALL APPEAL	Good	9	of possible	15
DESIGN & VARIETY	Average	6	of possible	15
SCENERY	Outstanding	15	of possible	15
OVERALL DIFFICULTY	Average	4	of possible	10
GREENS DIFFICULTY	Below Average	2	of possible	10
OVERALL CONDITION	Average	4	of possible	10
GREENS CONDITION	Average	4	of possible	10
HAZARDS	Good	6	of possible	10
COSMETICS	Below Average	1	of possible	5
TOTAL	**Average**	**51**	**of possible**	**100**

Description The front side of this course is completely different from the back side. The front side winds through sand dunes. Ice plant and sand dunes provide most of the hazards. There are some good holes with greens tucked near sand dunes. There are also some really short holes. Many elevated tee boxes give you beautiful ocean views. The back side has rolling hills with medium-wide fairways bordered by mature pine and eucalyptus trees. Residential housing surrounds the back side.

QUALITY RANKING 64th VALUE RANKING 65th
Clubhouse Facilities FAIR Pro shop, snack bar

Practice Facilities FAIR Driving range, putting green

Who Should Play Everyone

Walkability Moderate

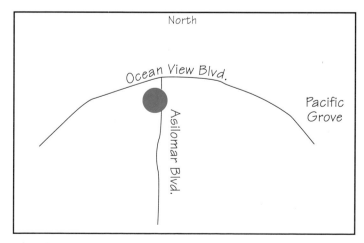

Directions *In Pacific Grove: Go west on Ocean View Boulevard. Go South on Asilomar Boulevard to the golf course.*

THE LINKS AT SPANISH BAY

☐	☐	☐	☐	☐	■	
Poor	Below Average	Average	Good	Very Good	Outstanding	

THE LINKS AT SPANISH BAY

Address	17 Mile Drive
City, Zip	Pebble Beach, 93953
Telephone	(408) 624–3811
Ownership	Resort
Weekday Fee	$75
Weekend Fee	$75
Twilight Fee	—

Men's Par	72
Men's Yardage	6078
Men's Rating	70.8
Women's Par	72
Women's Yardage	5287
Women's Rating	70.8
Championship Yardage	6820
Championship Rating	74.7

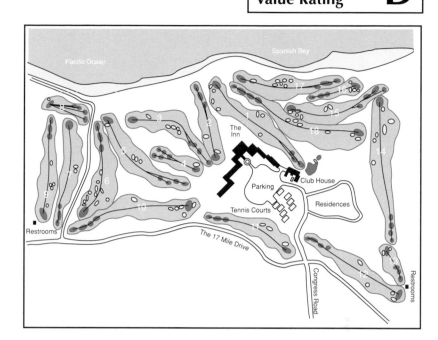

OVERALL APPEAL	Outstanding	15	of possible	15
DESIGN & VARIETY	Outstanding	15	of possible	15
SCENERY	Outstanding	15	of possible	15
OVERALL DIFFICULTY	Outstanding	10	of possible	10
GREENS DIFFICULTY	Outstanding	10	of possible	10
OVERALL CONDITION	Very Good	8	of possible	10
GREENS CONDITION	Average	4	of possible	10
HAZARDS	Outstanding	10	of possible	10
COSMETICS	Outstanding	5	of possible	5
TOTAL	**Outstanding**	**92**	**of possible**	**100**

Description There are a few holes that weave through the forest. Deep bunkers, mounds, marsh, sand dunes, barrancas, heather, ravines, and pine trees provide exceptional hazards. Also, many holes have beautiful ocean views. The course has a masterful design with stunning holes and plenty of challenge. 1st MOST DIFFICULT HAZARDS 1st MOST DIFFICULT GREENS 2nd MOST DIFFICULT COURSE 2nd BEST CLUB-HOUSE 3rd BEST DESIGN 3rd BEST FINISHING HOLE 4th BEST SCENERY 4th BEST SCORECARD 8th BEST COSMETICS

QUALITY RANKING 9th   VALUE RANKING 89th
Clubhouse Facilities EXCELLENT Pro shop, snack bar, coffee shop, full bar, fine dining, banquet
Practice Facilities GOOD Putting green, chipping green, bunker
Who Should Play Everyone, at least once; then those looking for a challenge
Walkability Moderate (carts are mandatory and must stay on paths)

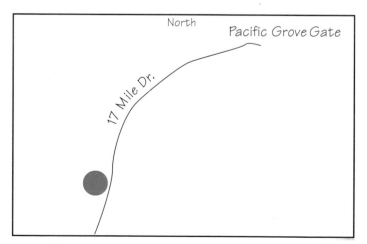

Directions *Go south on 17 Mile Drive from the Pacific Grove gate.*

☐	☐	☐	☐	☐	■
Poor	Below Average	Average	Good	Very Good	Outstanding

POPPY HILLS GOLF COURSE

Address   Lopez Road
City, Zip   Pebble Beach, 93953
Telephone   (408) 625–2154
Ownership   Independent
Weekday Fee $60
Weekend Fee $60
Twilight Fee   —

Men's Par   72
Men's Yardage   6219
Men's Rating   72.4
Women's Par   72
Women's Yardage   5326
Women's Rating   70.8
Championship
   Yardage   6850
Championship
   Rating   75.2

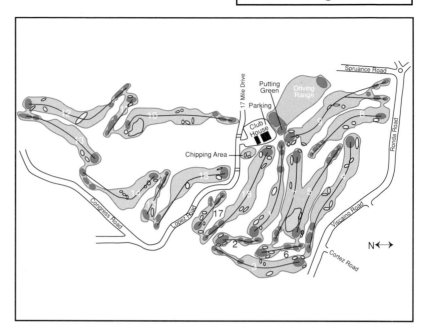

OVERALL APPEAL	Outstanding	15	of possible	15
DESIGN & VARIETY	Outstanding	15	of possible	15
SCENERY	Outstanding	15	of possible	15
OVERALL DIFFICULTY	Outstanding	10	of possible	10
GREENS DIFFICULTY	Outstanding	10	of possible	10
OVERALL CONDITION	Outstanding	10	of possible	10
GREENS CONDITION	Outstanding	10	of possible	10
HAZARDS	Outstanding	10	of possible	10
COSMETICS	Very Good	4	of possible	5
TOTAL	**Outstanding**	**99**	**of possible**	**100**

Description   This course is located in the beautiful Del Monte Forest. It has rolling hills with medium-wide fairways bordered by mature pine trees. Canyons, lakes, excellent bunkers, and trees provide the hazards. 2nd OVERALL CONDITION 2nd BEST GREENS CONDITION 3rd BEST SCENERY 3rd BEST HAZARDS 3rd MOST DIFFICULT COURSE 3rd MOST DIFFICULT GREENS 4th BEST DESIGN 5th BEST CLUBHOUSE 6th BEST PRACTICE FACILITIES 9th BEST SCORECARD

QUALITY RANKING 2nd   VALUE RANKING 80th
Clubhouse Facilities EXCELLENT Pro shop, coffee shop, full bar, snack bar
Practice Facilities EXCELLENT Driving range, 2 putting greens, bunker
Who Should Play Everyone
Walkability Moderate (NCGA members may walk but public must take carts and stay on paths)

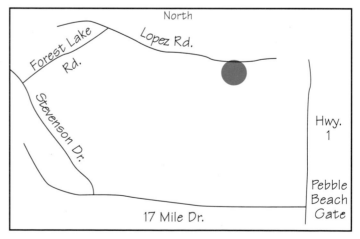

Directions *From Highway 1: Exit west on 17 Mile Drive from the Pebble Beach gate. Go north on Stevenson Drive. Go north on Forest Lake Road. Go east on Lopez Road to the golf course.*

SPYGLASS HILL GOLF COURSE

Poor	Below Average	Average	Good	Very Good	Outstanding
☐	☐	☐	☐	☐	■

Quality Rating 100

Value Rating D

SPYGLASS HILL GOLF COURSE

Address	P.O. Box 658
City, Zip	Pebble Beach, 93953
Telephone	(408) 624–3811
Ownership	Resort
Weekday Fee	$85
Weekend Fee	$85
Twilight Fee	$35

Men's Par	72
Men's Yardage	6277
Men's Rating	73.1
Women's Par	72
Women's Yardage	5556
Women's Rating	72.8
Championship Yardage	6810
Championship Rating	76.1

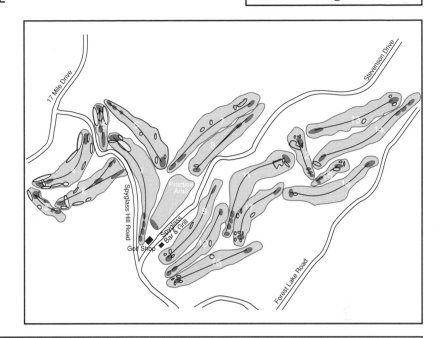

OVERALL APPEAL	Outstanding	15	of possible	15
DESIGN & VARIETY	Outstanding	15	of possible	15
SCENERY	Outstanding	15	of possible	15
OVERALL DIFFICULTY	Outstanding	10	of possible	10
GREENS DIFFICULTY	Outstanding	10	of possible	10
OVERALL CONDITION	Outstanding	10	of possible	10
GREENS CONDITION	Outstanding	10	of possible	10
HAZARDS	Outstanding	10	of possible	10
COSMETICS	Outstanding	5	of possible	5
TOTAL	**Outstanding**	**100**	**of possible**	**100**

Description This course has rolling hills with narrow to medium-wide fairways nestled in the Del Monte Forest. The first five holes are in the sand dunes near the ocean. Trees, small lakes, beautiful bunkers, ice plant, and sand dunes provide the hazards. It could be the closest to a perfect public golf course you can get. 1st BEST DESIGN 1st MOST DIFFICULT COURSE 1st BEST OVERALL CONDITION 1st BEST GREENS CONDITION 2nd BEST SCENERY 2nd MOST DIFFICULT GREENS 2nd BEST HAZARDS 2nd BEST SCORECARD 4th BEST COSMETICS

QUALITY RANKING 1st   VALUE RANKING 94th
Clubhouse Facilities   GOOD Pro shop, bar and grill
Practice Facilities   GOOD Driving range, putting green
Who Should Play Everyone, at least once; then, those looking for a challenge
Walkability Moderate

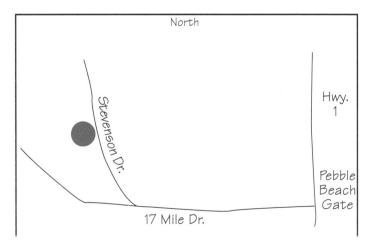

Directions *From Highway 1: Exit west on 17 mile Drive from the Pebble Beach gate. Go north on Stevenson Drive to the golf course.*

PEBBLE BEACH GOLF LINKS

Poor	Below Average	Average	Good	Very Good	Outstanding			

Quality Rating	98
Value Rating	F

PEBBLE BEACH GOLF LINKS

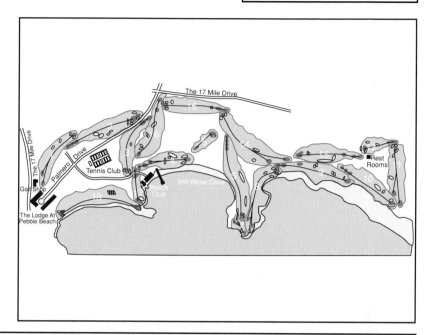

Address	17 Mile Drive
City, Zip	Pebble Beach, 93953
Telephone	(408) 624–3811
Ownership	Resort
Weekday Fee	$125
Weekend Fee	$125
Twilight Fee	—
Men's Par	72
Men's Yardage	6357
Men's Rating	72.7
Women's Par	72
Women's Yardage	5197
Women's Rating	70.3
Championship Yardage	6799
Championship Rating	75.0

OVERALL APPEAL	Outstanding	15	of possible	15
DESIGN & VARIETY	Outstanding	15	of possible	15
SCENERY	Outstanding	15	of possible	15
OVERALL DIFFICULTY	Outstanding	10	of possible	10
GREENS DIFFICULTY	Outstanding	10	of possible	10
OVERALL CONDITION	Very Good	8	of possible	10
GREENS CONDITION	Outstanding	10	of possible	10
HAZARDS	Outstanding	10	of possible	10
COSMETICS	Outstanding	5	of possible	5
TOTAL	**Outstanding**	**98**	**of possible**	**100**

Description This course has rolling hills with medium to wide fairways bordered by mature oak and pine trees. One side sits on the bluffs of Carmel Bay and the other side has beautiful homes. Large, contoured bunkers, ravines, and the Pacific Ocean provide most of the hazards. 1st BEST SCENERY 1st BEST FINISHING HOLE 1st BEST CLUBHOUSE 3rd BEST COSMETICS 3rd BEST SCORECARD 5th MOST DIFFICULT COURSE 5th MOST DIFFICULT GREENS 5th BEST GREENS CONDITION 6th BEST DESIGN 7th BEST OVERALL CONDITION 7th BEST HAZARDS

QUALITY RANKING 3rd   VALUE RANKING 107th
Clubhouse Facilities EXCELLENT Pro shop, coffee shop, full bar, fine dining, banquet
Practice Facilities FAIR Driving range, putting green, bunker
Who Should Play Everyone
Walkability Moderate (Caddies or carts are mandatory and must stay on paths)

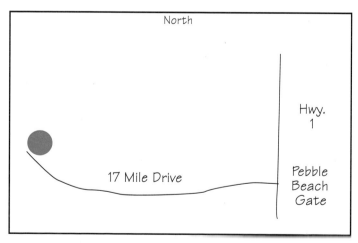

Directions *From Highway 1: Exit west on 17 Mile Drive at the Pebble Beach gate and continue to the golf course.*

RANCHO CAÑADA GOLF CLUB—WEST

Quality Rating	**70**
Value Rating	**D**

RANCHO CAÑADA GOLF CLUB
—WEST

Address	Carmel Valley Road
City, Zip	Carmel, 93922
Telephone	(408) 624–0111
Ownership	Independent
Weekday Fee	$34
Weekend Fee	$34
Twilight Fee	$18

Men's Par	72
Men's Yardage	6142
Men's Rating	69.5
Women's Par	73
Women's Yardage	5453
Women's Rating	70.5
Championship Yardage	6613
Championship Rating	72.3

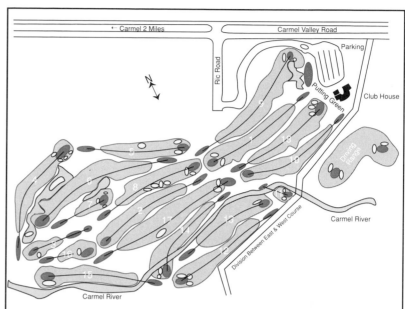

OVERALL APPEAL	Good	9	of possible	15
DESIGN & VARIETY	Good	9	of possible	15
SCENERY	Very Good	12	of possible	15
OVERALL DIFFICULTY	Very Good	8	of possible	10
GREENS DIFFICULTY	Good	6	of possible	10
OVERALL CONDITION	Average	4	of possible	10
GREENS CONDITION	Outstanding	10	of possible	10
HAZARDS	Very Good	8	of possible	10
COSMETICS	Very Good	4	of possible	5
TOTAL	**Good**	**70**	**of possible**	**100**

Description   This course is flat with a few hills. It has very narrow to medium-wide fairways bordered by middle-aged pine and mature cottonwood trees. It is located in Carmel Valley with foothills on one side and Carmel Valley Road on the other side. On the front side, the holes tend to play the same with slight doglegs and some water. The back side is more varied with holes crossing over the Carmel River. Some greens are nicely tucked behind huge cottonwood trees. 5th BEST PRACTICE FACILITIES 8th BEST GREENS CONDITION 9th BEST COSMETICS

QUALITY RANKING 33rd   VALUE RANKING 86th

Clubhouse Facilities   GOOD   Pro shop, snack bar, coffee shop, fine dining, banquet

Practice Facilities   EXCELLENT   Driving range, putting green, chipping green, 2 bunkers

Who Should Play   Everyone

Walkability   Moderate

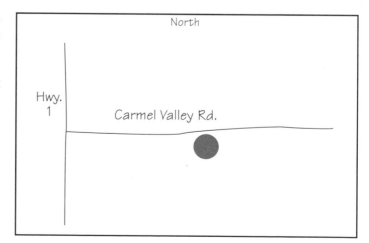

Directions   *From Highway 1: Go east on Carmel Valley Road about 1 mile to the golf course.*

RANCHO CAÑADA GOLF CLUB—EAST

						Quality Rating	**75**
Poor	Below Average	Average	Good	Very Good	Outstanding	Value Rating	**D**

RANCHO CAÑADA GOLF CLUB
—EAST

Address	Carmel Valley Road
City, Zip	Carmel, 93922
Telephone	(408) 624–0111
Ownership	Independent
Weekday Fee	$34
Weekend Fee	$34
Twilight Fee	$18

Men's Par	71
Men's Yardage	6034
Men's Rating	68.7
Women's Par	72
Women's Yardage	5255
Women's Rating	69.0
Championship Yardage	6434
Championship Rating	70.3

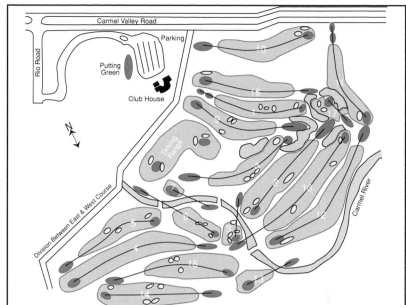

OVERALL APPEAL	Very Good	12	of possible	15
DESIGN & VARIETY	Very Good	12	of possible	15
SCENERY	Very Good	12	of possible	15
OVERALL DIFFICULTY	Good	6	of possible	10
GREENS DIFFICULTY	Good	6	of possible	10
OVERALL CONDITION	Average	4	of possible	10
GREENS CONDITION	Outstanding	10	of possible	10
HAZARDS	Very Good	8	of possible	10
COSMETICS	Outstanding	5	of possible	5
TOTAL	**Good**	**75**	**of possible**	**100**

Description   This course is flat with a few small hills. The fairways are narrow to medium-wide bordered by young to mature trees. Huge cottonwood trees, the Carmel River, many contoured bunkers, and some water provide the hazards. It's located in Carmel Valley with nice views of the Santa Lucia Mountains. It has interesting holes that are fun to play. Also, there are excellent par 3's that go over the Carmel River. 5th BEST PRACTICE FACILITIES 7th BEST COSMETICS 7th BEST GREENS CONDITION

QUALITY RANKING   28th   VALUE RANKING   82nd
Clubhouse Facilities   GOOD   Pro shop, snack bar, coffee shop, full bar, fine dining, banquet
Practice Facilities   EXCELLENT   Driving range, putting green, chipping green, 2 bunkers
Who Should Play   Everyone

Walkability   Moderate

Directions   *From Highway 1: Go east on Carmel Valley Road about 1 mile to the golf course.*

Poor	Below Average	Average	Good	Very Good	Outstanding
☐	☐	■	☐	☐	☐

Quality Rating	57
Value Rating	C

SALINAS FAIRWAYS GOLF COURSE

Address	45 Skyway Boulevard
City, Zip	Salinas, 93902
Telephone	(408) 758–7300
Ownership	Municipal
Weekday Fee	$10
Weekend Fee	$12.50
Twilight Fee	$7.50

Men's Par	72
Men's Yardage	6347
Men's Rating	68.8
Women's Par	73
Women's Yardage	5674
Women's Rating	70.8
Championship Yardage	6587
Championship Rating	69.9

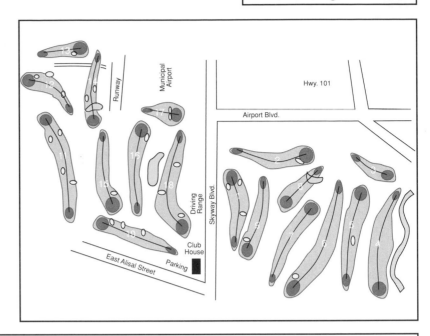

OVERALL APPEAL	Good	9	of possible	15
DESIGN & VARIETY	Good	9	of possible	15
SCENERY	Good	9	of possible	15
OVERALL DIFFICULTY	Good	6	of possible	10
GREENS DIFFICULTY	Good	6	of possible	10
OVERALL CONDITION	Good	6	of possible	10
GREENS CONDITION	Good	6	of possible	10
HAZARDS	Average	4	of possible	10
COSMETICS	Average	2	of possible	5
TOTAL	**Average**	**57**	**of possible**	**100**

Description The front side is completely different from the back side. The front side is flat with wide undulating fairways that are bordered by mature, majestic pine trees. Many of these holes are sweeping doglegs. The back side is completely wide open with some water and bunkers providing the hazards. The entire course is surrounded by residential housing and the Salinas Airport.

QUALITY RANKING 50th   VALUE RANKING 38th
Clubhouse Facilities   FAIR Pro shop, snack bar

Practice Facilities   FAIR Driving range, putting green

Who Should Play Everyone

Walkability Easy

Directions *From Highway 101: Exit east on Airport Boulevard. Go north on Skyway Boulevard to the golf course.*

☐	☐	☐	■	☐	☐
Poor	Below Average	Average	Good	Very Good	Outstanding

RIDGEMARK COUNTRY CLUB —GABILAN

Address	3800 Airline Highway
City, Zip	Hollister, 95023
Telephone	(408) 637–1010
Ownership	Resort
Weekday Fee	$15
Weekend Fee	$20
Twilight Fee	$8

Men's Par	72
Men's Yardage	6271
Men's Rating	69.4
Women's Par	72
Women's Yardage	5670
Women's Rating	70.8
Championship Yardage	6771
Championship Rating	71.7

OVERALL APPEAL	Very Good	12	of possible	15
DESIGN & VARIETY	Very Good	12	of possible	15
SCENERY	Very Good	12	of possible	15
OVERALL DIFFICULTY	Very Good	8	of possible	10
GREENS DIFFICULTY	Very Good	8	of possible	10
OVERALL CONDITION	Very Good	8	of possible	10
GREENS CONDITION	Average	4	of possible	10
HAZARDS	Very Good	8	of possible	10
COSMETICS	Very Good	4	of possible	5
TOTAL	**Good**	**76**	**of possible**	**100**

Description   The front side is new. It weaves through residential housing with medium to wide fairways bordered by very young trees. It's nicely designed and fun to play. There are bunkers, some water, and many mounds surrounding the greens. Some holes have panoramic views of the foothills. The back side is more established with much larger trees. Trees, bunkers, and a ravine provide the hazards. Overall, this course is very enjoyable to play. 7th BEST CLUBHOUSE 10th BEST OVERALL CONDITION

QUALITY RANKING   25th   VALUE RANKING   27th
Clubhouse Facilities   EXCELLENT   Pro shop, snack bar, coffee shop, full bar, fine dining, banquet
Practice Facilities   FAIR   Driving range, putting green, chipping green
Who Should Play   Everyone

Walkability   Moderate

North

Hollister

Hwy. 25

Ridgemark Dr.

Directions   *From downtown Hollister: Go south on Highway 25 about 3 miles. Go south on Ridgemark Drive to the course.*

RIDGEMARK COUNTRY CLUB—DIABLO

Poor	Below Average	Average	Good	Very Good	Outstanding
☐	☐	☐	☐	■	☐

Quality Rating 83

Value Rating A

RIDGEMARK COUNTRY CLUB—DIABLO

Address	3800 Airline Highway
City, Zip	Hollister, 95023
Telephone	(408) 637–1010
Ownership	Resort
Weekday Fee	$15
Weekend Fee	$20
Twilight Fee	$8

Men's Par	72
Men's Yardage	6032
Men's Rating	68.3
Women's Par	72
Women's Yardage	5427
Women's Rating	70.5
Championship Yardage	6603
Championship Rating	70.9

OVERALL APPEAL	Outstanding	15	of possible	15
DESIGN & VARIETY	Outstanding	15	of possible	15
SCENERY	Outstanding	15	of possible	15
OVERALL DIFFICULTY	Very Good	8	of possible	10
GREENS DIFFICULTY	Good	6	of possible	10
OVERALL CONDITION	Outstanding	10	of possible	10
GREENS CONDITION	Average	4	of possible	10
HAZARDS	Good	6	of possible	10
COSMETICS	Very Good	4	of possible	5
TOTAL	**Very Good**	**83**	**of possible**	**100**

Description This course has rolling hills, with a few steep ones. Fairways are medium-wide bordered by very young to middle-aged trees. There are beautiful, panoramic views of the surrounding countryside. Trees, water, bunkers, a ravine, and out-of-bounds provide the hazards. Some holes are from the old course with more traditional design. The other holes are newly designed and much more exciting to play. 4th BEST OVERALL CONDITION 7th BEST CLUBHOUSE

QUALITY RANKING 15th **VALUE RANKING** 10th

Clubhouse Facilities **EXCELLENT** Pro shop, snack bar, coffee shop, full bar, fine dining, banquet

Practice Facilities **FAIR** Driving range, putting green, chipping green

Who Should Play Everyone

Walkability Difficult

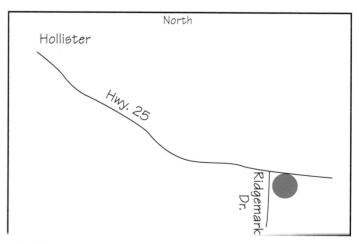

Directions *From downtown Hollister: Go south on Highway 25 about 3 miles. Go south on Ridgemark Drive to the course.*

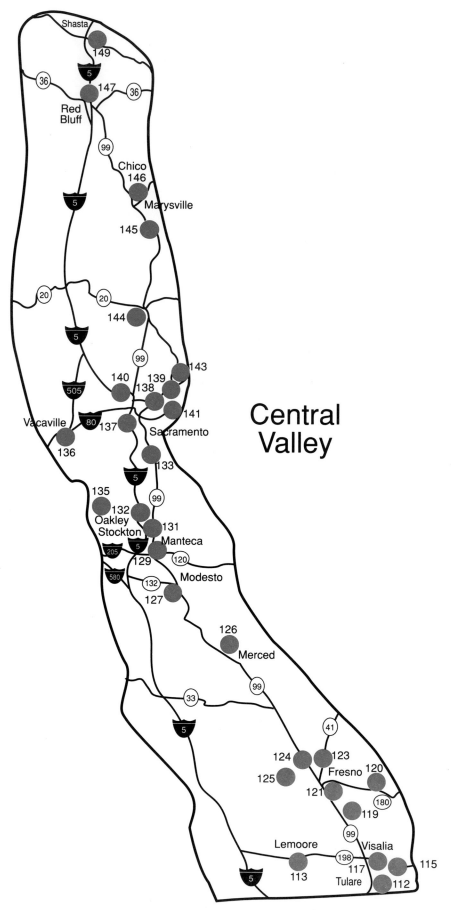

Central
Valley

Numbered dots indicate the page number where the golf course is described.

CENTRAL VALLEY

The San Joaquin and Sacramento valleys are flat with cities and towns scattered around. It is a region made up of hundreds of square miles of farmlands. This zone covers an area from the Coastal Range in the west to the base of the Sierra Nevada foothills in the east and from the city of Redding in the north to the town of Tulare in the south.

With a few exceptions, most of these courses are flat and tend to look the same. This zone offers the least expensive golfing in Northern California. Almost all the courses are of average quality.

Weather changes dramatically from season to season. Fog can set in each winter so that you might not see the sun for several days. This limits visibility and golfing for all but the most die-hard golfer. In the summer, the temperature can go well over 100 degrees in the afternoon, making early mornings and late afternoons the preferable time to play. Spring and fall are the best times of the year to enjoy the golf courses in this zone.

Municipal/county golf courses are very inexpensive. Unfortunately, many of them are very crowded and not maintained as well as they should be. Dress code is definitely informal. On weekends and mornings you should make a tee time prior to playing.

Most independent courses in this zone are moderately priced. Maintenance conditions range from poor to very good. Tee times aren't necessary at many of the courses. The dress code is informal.

There are no public, resort golf courses in the Central Valley.

Poor	Below Average	Average	Good	Very Good	Outstanding
☐	☐	■	☐	☐	☐

Quality Rating **41**

Value Rating **C**

TULARE GOLF COURSE

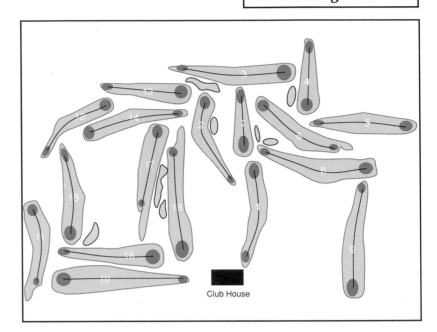

Club House

Address	5320 S. Laspina Street
City, Zip	Tulare, 93274
Telephone	(209) 686–9839
Ownership	Independent
Weekday Fee	$8
Weekend Fee	$11
Twilight Fee	—

Men's Par	72
Men's Yardage	6534
Men's Rating	69.5
Women's Par	72
Women's Yardage	5626
Women's Rating	70.5
Championship Yardage	6734
Championship Rating	70.5

OVERALL APPEAL	Average	6	of possible	15
DESIGN & VARIETY	Average	6	of possible	15
SCENERY	Below Average	3	of possible	15
OVERALL DIFFICULTY	Good	6	of possible	10
GREENS DIFFICULTY	Good	6	of possible	10
OVERALL CONDITION	Average	4	of possible	10
GREENS CONDITION	Average	4	of possible	10
HAZARDS	Average	4	of possible	10
COSMETICS	Average	2	of possible	5
TOTAL	**Average**	**41**	**of possible**	**100**

Description   This course is flat with medium-wide fairways bordered by young to middle-aged oak and eucalyptus trees. It is surrounded by farmland. Bunkers and some water provide the hazards. Most of the holes tend to look the same. Some greens are two-tiered and fun to putt. Also, greens are slightly elevated from the fairways.

QUALITY RANKING   87th   VALUE RANKING   50th
Clubhouse Facilities   GOOD   Pro shop, coffee shop, full bar
Practice Facilities   GOOD   Driving range, 2 putting greens, chipping green, bunker
Who Should Play   Everyone

Walkability   Easy

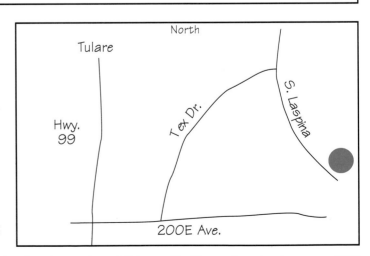

Directions   *From Highway 99: Go south and exit east on 200E Avenue. Go north on Tex Drive. Go south on S. Laspina to the golf course.*

Poor	Below Average	Average	Good	Very Good	Outstanding

Quality Rating	**9**
Value Rating	**F**

JACKSON LAKES GOLF COURSE

Address	14868 18th Avenue
City, Zip	Lemoore, 93245
Telephone	(209) 924–2763
Ownership	Independent
Weekday Fee	$5
Weekend Fee	$6
Twilight Fee	$4

Men's Par	71
Men's Yardage	5677
Men's Rating	67.9
Women's Par	71
Women's Yardage	5384
Women's Rating	66.0
Championship Yardage	6010
Championship Rating	69.0

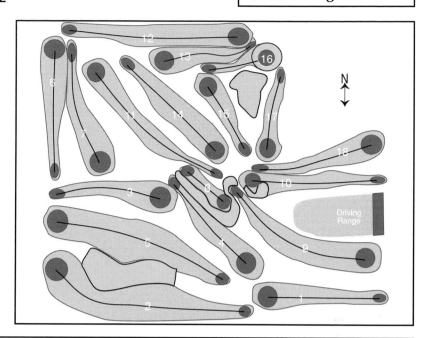

OVERALL APPEAL	Poor	0	of possible	15
DESIGN & VARIETY	Below Average	3	of possible	15
SCENERY	Poor	0	of possible	15
OVERALL DIFFICULTY	Below Average	2	of possible	10
GREENS DIFFICULTY	Poor	0	of possible	10
OVERALL CONDITION	Poor	0	of possible	10
GREENS CONDITION	Below Average	2	of possible	10
HAZARDS	Below Average	2	of possible	10
COSMETICS	Poor	0	of possible	5
TOTAL	**Poor**	**9**	**of possible**	**100**

Description   This course is flat with medium to wide fairways bordered by young trees. It is surrounded by farmland. Bunkers and some water provide the hazards. Most of the holes are very boring. However, there are a few decent holes where water comes into play. Unfortunately, an unbelievable lack of maintenance makes this golf course unplayable.

QUALITY RANKING 112th VALUE RANKING 111th

Clubhouse Facilities   POOR   Pro shop, snack bar

Practice Facilities   FAIR   Driving range, putting green

Who Should Play   Those looking for convenience

Walkability   Easy

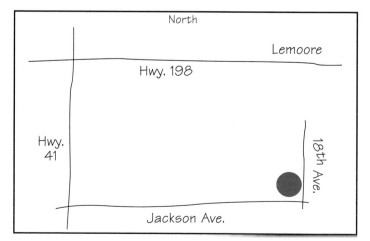

Directions   *From Highway 198: Go south on Highway 41 about 3 miles. Go east on Jackson Avenue to the golf course.*

SIERRA VIEW GOLF COURSE

Quality Rating **27**

Value Rating **D**

SIERRA VIEW GOLF COURSE

Address	12608 Avenue 604
City, Zip	Visalia, 93277
Telephone	(209) 732–2078
Ownership	Independent
Weekday Fee	$7.50
Weekend Fee	$9
Twilight Fee	—

Men's Par	72
Men's Yardage	6465
Men's Rating	68.4
Women's Par	73
Women's Yardage	5809
Women's Rating	72.1
Championship Yardage	—
Championship Rating	—

OVERALL APPEAL	Below Average	3	of possible	15
DESIGN & VARIETY	Below Average	3	of possible	15
SCENERY	Below Average	3	of possible	15
OVERALL DIFFICULTY	Average	4	of possible	10
GREENS DIFFICULTY	Average	4	of possible	10
OVERALL CONDITION	Below Average	2	of possible	10
GREENS CONDITION	Average	4	of possible	10
HAZARDS	Below Average	2	of possible	10
COSMETICS	Average	2	of possible	5
TOTAL	**Below Average**	**27**	**of possible**	**100**

Description   This golf course is flat with medium-wide fairways bordered by young to middle-aged pine, oak, and eucalyptus trees. The front side is surrounded by farmland and the back side has residential housing around it.

QUALITY RANKING 105th   VALUE RANKING 93rd

Clubhouse Facilities   FAIR Pro shop, snack bar, full bar

Practice Facilities   FAIR 2 putting greens, driving range, sand trap

Who Should Play Those looking for convenience

Walkability Easy

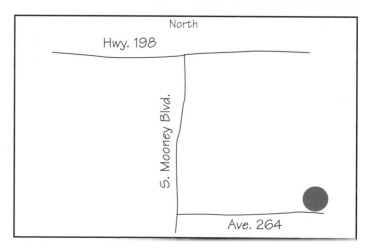

Directions   *From Highway 198: Exit south on Mooney Boulevard about 4½ miles. Go east on Avenue 264 to the golf course.*

VALLEY OAKS GOLF COURSE

Poor	Below Average	Average	Good	Very Good	Outstanding
☐	☐	■	☐	☐	☐

VALLEY OAKS GOLF COURSE

Address	1800 South Plaza Drive
City, Zip	Visalia, 93277
Telephone	(209) 651–1441
Ownership	Municipal
Weekday Fee	$8
Weekend Fee	$9.50
Twilight Fee	—

Men's Par	72
Men's Yardage	6250
Men's Rating	68.2
Women's Par	72
Women's Yardage	5746
Women's Rating	72.4
Championship Yardage	6469
Championship Rating	69.6

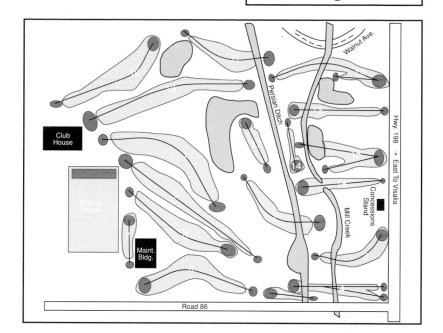

OVERALL APPEAL	Average	6	of possible	15
DESIGN & VARIETY	Good	9	of possible	15
SCENERY	Average	6	of possible	15
OVERALL DIFFICULTY	Average	4	of possible	10
GREENS DIFFICULTY	Good	6	of possible	10
OVERALL CONDITION	Average	4	of possible	10
GREENS CONDITION	Good	6	of possible	10
HAZARDS	Average	4	of possible	10
COSMETICS	Average	2	of possible	5
TOTAL	**Average**	**47**	**of possible**	**100**

Description This course is flat with narrow to wide fairways bordered by young to mature oak, pine, and eucalyptus trees. It is surrounded by the highway, farmland, and the Visalia Airport. Trees, water, and bunkers provide the hazards. There are lots of doglegs and some very interesting holes. The overall appeal of this course could be raised if the water hazards had more water in them.

QUALITY RANKING 72nd VALUE RANKING 35th
Clubhouse Facilities GOOD Pro shop, snack bar, full bar
Practice Facilities GOOD Driving range, putting green, chipping green, bunker
Who Should Play Everyone

Walkability Easy

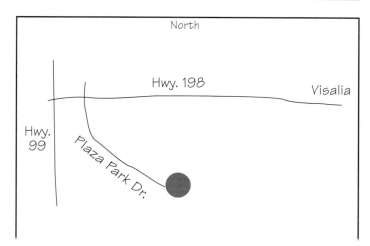

Directions *From downtown Visalia: Go west on Highway 198 about 5 miles. Exit south on Plaza Park Drive to the course.*

SELMA VALLEY GOLF COURSE

Poor	Below Average	Average	Good	Very Good	Outstanding
☐	■	☐	☐	☐	☐

Quality Rating **38**

Value Rating **D**

SELMA VALLEY GOLF COURSE

Address	12389 E. Rose Avenue
City, Zip	Selma, 93662
Telephone	(209) 896–2424
Ownership	Independent
Weekday Fee	$9
Weekend Fee	$12
Twilight Fee	—

Men's Par	69
Men's Yardage	5349
Men's Rating	64.3
Women's Par	70
Women's Yardage	5072
Women's Rating	67.2
Championship Yardage	—
Championship Rating	—

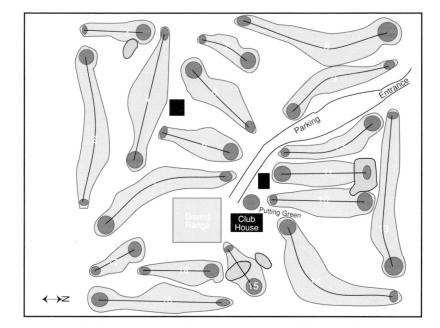

OVERALL APPEAL	Average	6	of possible	15
DESIGN & VARIETY	Below Average	3	of possible	15
SCENERY	Average	6	of possible	15
OVERALL DIFFICULTY	Below Average	2	of possible	10
GREENS DIFFICULTY	Average	4	of possible	10
OVERALL CONDITION	Average	4	of possible	10
GREENS CONDITION	Very Good	8	of possible	10
HAZARDS	Average	4	of possible	10
COSMETICS	Below Average	1	of possible	5
TOTAL	**Below Average**	**38**	**of possible**	**100**

Description This course is flat with a few small hills. Fairways are medium-wide and bordered by middle-aged pine, oak, poplar, eucalyptus, and palm trees. Bunkers and some water provide additional hazards. Most of the holes play very short. Bunkers are strategically placed to provide easy or difficult pin placements. There are some interesting views of the surrounding vineyards.

QUALITY RANKING 93rd   VALUE RANKING 84th
Clubhouse Facilities   POOR   Pro shop, snack bar

Practice Facilities   POOR   Driving range, putting green

Who Should Play   Beginners

Walkability   Moderate

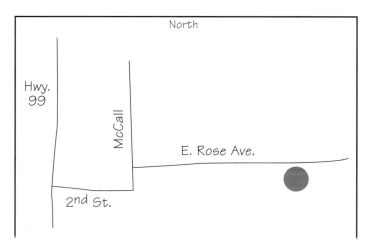

Directions   *From Highway 99: Exit east on 2nd Street. Go north on McCall and immediately go east on E. Rose Avenue about 2 miles to the golf course.*

119

Poor	Below Average	■ Average	Good	Very Good	Outstanding

SHERWOOD FOREST GOLF CLUB

Address	79 N. Frankwood Avenue
City, Zip	Sanger, 93657
Telephone	(209) 787–2611
Ownership	Independent
Weekday Fee	$9
Weekend Fee	$11
Twilight Fee	—

Men's Par	71
Men's Yardage	6160
Men's Rating	68.4
Women's Par	72
Women's Yardage	5555
Women's Rating	68.5
Championship Yardage	—
Championship Rating	—

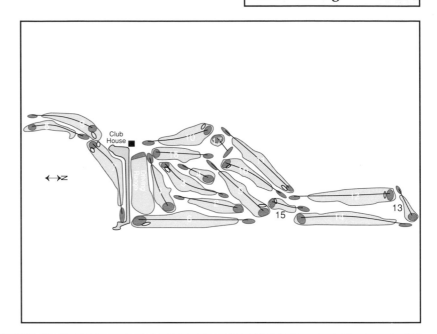

OVERALL APPEAL	Good	9	of possible	15
DESIGN & VARIETY	Average	6	of possible	15
SCENERY	Good	9	of possible	15
OVERALL DIFFICULTY	Average	4	of possible	10
GREENS DIFFICULTY	Average	4	of possible	10
OVERALL CONDITION	Average	4	of possible	10
GREENS CONDITION	Good	6	of possible	10
HAZARDS	Good	6	of possible	10
COSMETICS	Good	3	of possible	5
TOTAL	**Average**	**51**	**of possible**	**100**

Description This course is flat with narrow to wide fairways bordered by young to mature pine, oak, and eucalyptus trees. Some water, trees, and high-lipped bunkers provide the hazards. One side is bordered by the Kings River and the other side has foothills. The holes alongside the river are narrow with very large trees. The other holes are generally wide open with much smaller trees. It is a fun course to play. Management shows some pride at this golf course.

QUALITY RANKING 66th   VALUE RANKING 39th

Clubhouse Facilities FAIR Pro shop, snack bar, banquet

Practice Facilities FAIR Driving range, 2 putting greens, bunker

Who Should Play Everyone

Walkability Easy

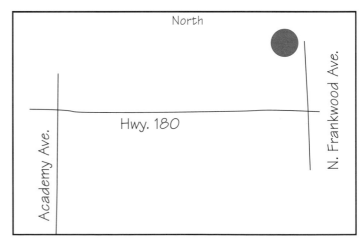

Directions *From downtown Selma: Go north on Academy Avenue. Go east on Highway 180 about 6½ miles. Go north on N. Frankwood Avenue about 1 mile to the golf course.*

Quality Rating 25

Value Rating D

AIRWAYS PUBLIC GOLF COURSE

Address	5440 E. Shields Avenue
City, Zip	Fresno, 93727
Telephone	(209) 291–6254
Ownership	Municipal
Weekday Fee	$6
Weekend Fee	$7
Twilight Fee	$4.75

Men's Par	68
Men's Yardage	5182
Men's Rating	63.8
Women's Par	70
Women's Yardage	5145
Women's Rating	67.9
Championship Yardage	—
Championship Rating	—

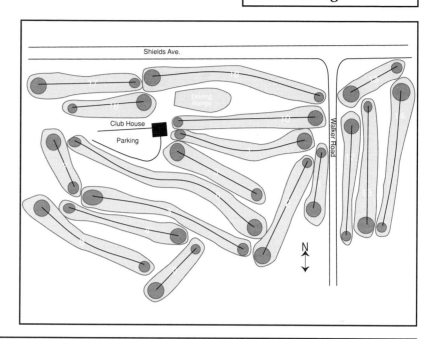

OVERALL APPEAL	Below Average	3	of possible	15
DESIGN & VARIETY	Below Average	3	of possible	15
SCENERY	Below Average	3	of possible	15
OVERALL DIFFICULTY	Below Average	2	of possible	10
GREENS DIFFICULTY	Average	4	of possible	10
OVERALL CONDITION	Poor	0	of possible	10
GREENS CONDITION	Average	4	of possible	10
HAZARDS	Good	6	of possible	10
COSMETICS	Poor	0	of possible	5
TOTAL	**Below Average**	**25**	**of possible**	**100**

Description This course is flat with narrow fairways bordered by middle-aged to mature oak and pine trees. It is located adjacent to the Fresno Airport and has commercial buildings on the other side. Trees, bunkers, oleander bushes, and out-of-bounds provide the hazards. Most of the holes play very short. Emphasis is on accurate driving off the tee. High-lipped bunkers make it next to impossible to chip the ball close to the pin. The maintenance leaves much to be desired.

QUALITY RANKING 108th   VALUE RANKING 85th

Clubhouse Facilities   POOR   Pro shop, snack bar

Practice Facilities   POOR   Driving range, putting green

Who Should Play   Those looking for convenience

Walkability   Easy

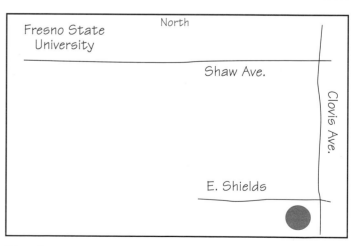

Directions   *From Fresno State University: Go east on Shaw Avenue about 3 miles. Go south on Clovis Avenue about 2 miles. Go west on E. Shields to the golf course.*

FIG GARDEN GOLF CLUB

| Poor | Below Average | Average | **Good** | Very Good | Outstanding |

	72
Quality Rating	
Value Rating	**B**

FIG GARDEN GOLF CLUB

Address	7700 N. Van Ness Boulevard
City, Zip	Fresno, 93711
Telephone	(209) 439-2928
Ownership	Independent
Weekday Fee	$15
Weekend Fee	$20
Twilight Fee	$10

Men's Par	72
Men's Yardage	6277
Men's Rating	69.0
Women's Par	72
Women's Yardage	5686
Women's Rating	72.0
Championship Yardage	6610
Championship Rating	70.0

OVERALL APPEAL	Very Good	12	of possible	15
DESIGN & VARIETY	Outstanding	15	of possible	15
SCENERY	Good	9	of possible	15
OVERALL DIFFICULTY	Good	6	of possible	10
GREENS DIFFICULTY	Good	6	of possible	10
OVERALL CONDITION	Good	6	of possible	10
GREENS CONDITION	Good	6	of possible	10
HAZARDS	Very Good	8	of possible	10
COSMETICS	Very Good	4	of possible	5
TOTAL	**Good**	**72**	**of possible**	**100**

Description   This course is flat with narrow to wide fairways bordered by a mixture of oak, pine, eucalyptus, and many other middle-aged to mature trees. It is bordered by the San Joaquin River on one side and beautiful homes high on a bluff on the other side. Trees, bunkers, and some water provide the hazards. It is a fun course to play with an exceptionally fine design for the valley. Management shows a lot of pride at this golf course. 6th BEST FINISHING HOLE

QUALITY RANKING   31st   VALUE RANKING   30th
Clubhouse Facilities   FAIR   Pro shop, snack bar, full bar
Practice Facilities   GOOD   Matted driving range, putting green, chipping green
Who Should Play   Everyone

Walkability   Easy

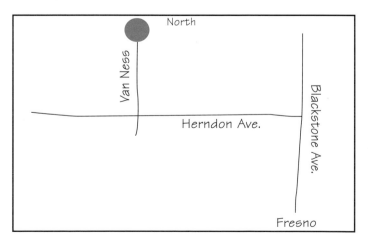

Directions   *From downtown Fresno: Go north on Blackstone Avenue. Go west on Herndon Avenue about 2 miles. Go north on Van Ness to the golf course.*

Poor	Below Average	Average	Good	Very Good	Outstanding
☐	☐	■	☐	☐	☐

RIVERSIDE GOLF COURSE

Address	7672 N. Josephine Avenue
City, Zip	Fresno, 93711
Telephone	(209) 275–5900
Ownership	Municipal
Weekday Fee	$6
Weekend Fee	$7
Twilight Fee	$4.75

Men's Par	72
Men's Yardage	6505
Men's Rating	70.8
Women's Par	75
Women's Yardage	6167
Women's Rating	73.0
Championship Yardage	6985
Championship Rating	71.6

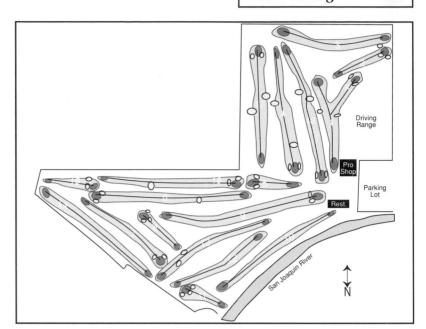

OVERALL APPEAL	Good	9	of possible	15
DESIGN & VARIETY	Very Good	12	of possible	15
SCENERY	Average	6	of possible	15
OVERALL DIFFICULTY	Very Good	8	of possible	10
GREENS DIFFICULTY	Good	6	of possible	10
OVERALL CONDITION	Below Average	2	of possible	10
GREENS CONDITION	Average	4	of possible	10
HAZARDS	Average	4	of possible	10
COSMETICS	Below Average	1	of possible	5
TOTAL	**Average**	**52**	**of possible**	**100**

Description   This course is flat with some small hills. Fairways are medium-wide bordered by middle-aged oak, pine, and eucalyptus trees. The San Joaquin River is on one side and farmland surrounds the other side. Trees, high-lipped bunkers, and many mounds in the fairways provide the hazards. There are a few very interesting holes that are in the small hills alongside the San Joaquin River. It could be a much better course with proper maintenance.

QUALITY RANKING   62nd   VALUE RANKING   15th
Clubhouse Facilities   FAIR   Pro shop, snack bar

Practice Facilities   GOOD   Driving range, 2 putting
greens, chipping green, bunker
Who Should Play   Everyone

Walkability   Moderate

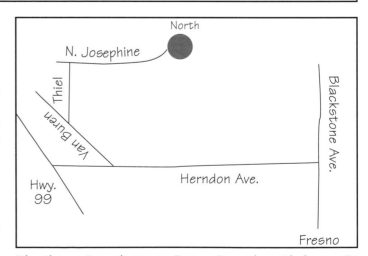

Directions   *From downtown Fresno: Go north on Blackstone. Go west on Herndon about 7 miles. Go north on Van Buren. Go north on Thiel. Go east on N. Josephine to the golf course.*

Poor	Below Average	Average	Good	Very Good	Outstanding
☐	☐	■	☐	☐	☐

Quality Rating	**47**
Value Rating	**C**

FRESNO WEST GOLF AND COUNTRY CLUB

Address	23986 Whitesbridge Road
City, Zip	Kerman, 93630
Telephone	(209) 846–8655
Ownership	Independent
Weekday Fee	$8.50
Weekend Fee	$11
Twilight Fee	—

Men's Par	72
Men's Yardage	6607
Men's Rating	70.2
Women's Par	73
Women's Yardage	5945
Women's Rating	72.8
Championship Yardage	6959
Championship Rating	71.8

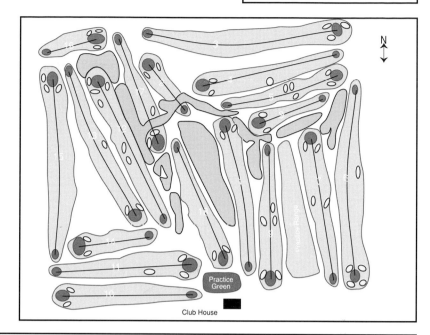

OVERALL APPEAL	Average	6	of possible	15
DESIGN & VARIETY	Average	6	of possible	15
SCENERY	Below Average	3	of possible	15
OVERALL DIFFICULTY	Very Good	8	of possible	10
GREENS DIFFICULTY	Good	6	of possible	10
OVERALL CONDITION	Good	6	of possible	10
GREENS CONDITION	Good	6	of possible	10
HAZARDS	Average	4	of possible	10
COSMETICS	Average	2	of possible	5
TOTAL	**Average**	**47**	**of possible**	**100**

Description   This course is flat with wide fairways bordered by young to middle-aged pine and eucalyptus trees. Bunkers and lakes provide most of the hazards. It is surrounded by farmland. It is a long course with plenty of room to swing away. There are some nice lakes that come into play. However, most of the holes tend to play the same. Management shows some pride here.

QUALITY RANKING   73rd   VALUE RANKING   42nd

Clubhouse Facilities   FAIR   Pro shop, snack bar, full bar

Practice Facilities   FAIR   Driving range, putting green, bunker

Who Should Play   Everyone

Walkability   Easy

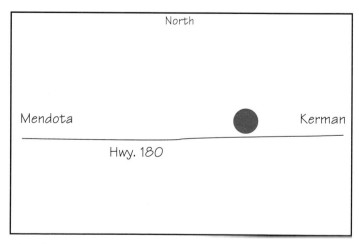

Directions   *From Kerman: Go west on Highway 180 about 8 miles to the golf course.*

Quality Rating	**48**
Value Rating	**C**

RANCHO DEL REY GOLF CLUB

Address	5250 Green Sands Avenue
City, Zip	Atwater, 95301
Telephone	(209) 358–7131
Ownership	Independent
Weekday Fee	$12
Weekend Fee	$16
Twilight Fee	$7

Men's Par	72
Men's Yardage	6262
Men's Rating	68.8
Women's Par	75
Women's Yardage	5856
Women's Rating	—
Championship Yardage	6712
Championship Rating	70.8

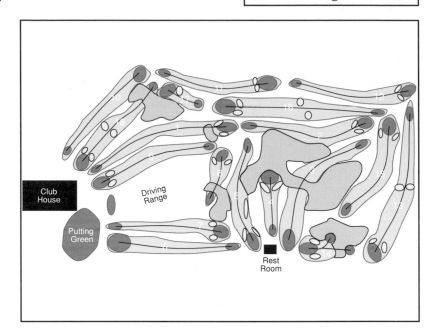

OVERALL APPEAL	Good	9	of possible	15
DESIGN & VARIETY	Good	9	of possible	15
SCENERY	Average	6	of possible	15
OVERALL DIFFICULTY	Good	6	of possible	10
GREENS DIFFICULTY	Average	4	of possible	10
OVERALL CONDITION	Below Average	2	of possible	10
GREENS CONDITION	Average	4	of possible	10
HAZARDS	Good	6	of possible	10
COSMETICS	Average	2	of possible	5
TOTAL	**Average**	**48**	**of possible**	**100**

Description   This course is flat with medium-wide fairways bordered by young to mature oak, pine, and eucalyptus trees. Trees, small bunkers, and some water provide the hazards. It is bordered by farmland. This course can be fun to play with a few interesting holes. There are plenty of subtle doglegs. Also there are strategically placed water hazards.

QUALITY RANKING   70th   VALUE RANKING   69th
Clubhouse Facilities   FAIR   Pro shop, snack bar, full bar
Practice Facilities   GOOD   Driving range, putting green
Who Should Play   Everyone

Walkability   Easy

126

Directions   *From Highway 99: Exit east on Buhach Avenue. Immediately go north on Green Sands Avenue to the golf course.*

Poor	Below Average	■ Average	Good	Very Good	Outstanding

DRYDEN PARK MUNICIPAL GOLF COURSE

Address	920 Sunset Boulevard
City, Zip	Modesto, 95351
Telephone	(209) 577–5359
Ownership	Municipal
Weekday Fee	$6
Weekend Fee	$7
Twilight Fee	$4

Men's Par	72
Men's Yardage	6140
Men's Rating	68.3
Women's Par	73
Women's Yardage	5888
Women's Rating	72.5
Championship Yardage	6514
Championship Rating	69.8

OVERALL APPEAL	Average	6	of possible	15
DESIGN & VARIETY	Average	6	of possible	15
SCENERY	Below Average	3	of possible	15
OVERALL DIFFICULTY	Average	4	of possible	10
GREENS DIFFICULTY	Average	4	of possible	10
OVERALL CONDITION	Good	6	of possible	10
GREENS CONDITION	Average	4	of possible	10
HAZARDS	Good	6	of possible	10
COSMETICS	Below Average	1	of possible	5
TOTAL	**Average**	**40**	**of possible**	**100**

Description This course is flat with a few small hills. Fairways are medium to wide bordered by middle-aged trees. The course is surrounded on one side by the Tuolumne River and an industrial area is on the other side. Trees, bunkers, and the Tuolumne River provide the hazards. It is typical of the San Joaquin Valley golf courses. There is nothing exciting about this course. However, there are a few interesting holes that are fun to play.

QUALITY RANKING 88th **VALUE RANKING** 29th

Clubhouse Facilities **FAIR** Pro shop, snack bar

Practice Facilities **FAIR** Driving range, 2 putting greens

Who Should Play Everyone

Walkability Easy

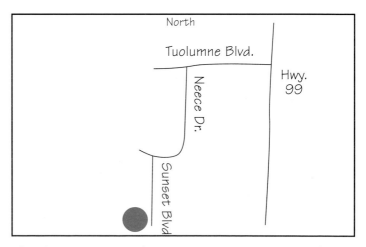

Directions *From Highway 99: Exit west on Tuolumne Boulevard. Go south on Neece Drive. Go south on Sunset Boulevard to the golf course.*

MANTECA PARK GOLF COURSE

MANTECA PARK GOLF COURSE

Address	305 N. Union Road
City, Zip	Manteca, 95336
Telephone	(209) 823–5945
Ownership	Municipal
Weekday Fee	$7.50
Weekend Fee	$8.50
Twilight Fee	—

Men's Par	72
Men's Yardage	6215
Men's Rating	69.3
Women's Par	72
Women's Yardage	5609
Women's Rating	71.5
Championship Yardage	6542
Championship Rating	70.7

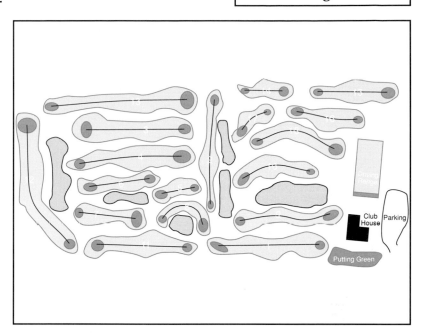

OVERALL APPEAL	Good	9	of possible	15
DESIGN & VARIETY	Good	9	of possible	15
SCENERY	Below Average	3	of possible	15
OVERALL DIFFICULTY	Good	6	of possible	10
GREENS DIFFICULTY	Average	4	of possible	10
OVERALL CONDITION	Good	6	of possible	10
GREENS CONDITION	Good	6	of possible	10
HAZARDS	Very Good	8	of possible	10
COSMETICS	Good	3	of possible	5
TOTAL	**Average**	**54**	**of possible**	**100**

Description This golf course is flat with a few mounds. Fairways are bordered by young to middle-aged pine, oak, and eucalyptus trees. Residential housing borders one side and farmland is on the other side. Trees, out-of-bounds, bunkers, and strategically placed lakes provide the hazards. The lakes and interesting design give this course some character. Also, management obviously takes pride in their facilities, making this course fun to play.

QUALITY RANKING 54th   VALUE RANKING 23rd
Clubhouse Facilities   FAIR   Pro shop, snack bar

Practice Facilities   FAIR   Driving range, 2 putting greens

Who Should Play   Everyone

Walkability   Easy

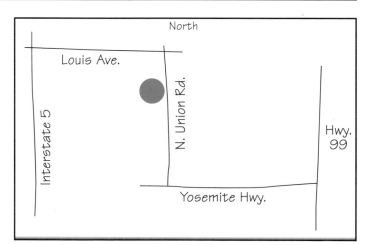

Directions   *From Highway 99: Exit west on Yosemite Highway through downtown Manteca. Go north on N. Union Road to the golf course.*

VAN BUSKIRK PARK GOLF COURSE

Poor	Below Average	Average	Good	Very Good	Outstanding
☐	☐	■	☐	☐	☐

VAN BUSKIRK PARK GOLF COURSE

Address	1740 Houston Avenue
City, Zip	Stockton, 95206
Telephone	(209) 464–5629
Ownership	Municipal
Weekday Fee	$6.50
Weekend Fee	$7.50
Twilight Fee	$5.50
Men's Par	72
Men's Yardage	6572
Men's Rating	69.7
Women's Par	74
Women's Yardage	6172
Women's Rating	73.6
Championship Yardage	—
Championship Rating	—

San Joaquin River

OVERALL APPEAL	Average	6	of possible	15
DESIGN & VARIETY	Good	9	of possible	15
SCENERY	Below Average	3	of possible	15
OVERALL DIFFICULTY	Good	6	of possible	10
GREENS DIFFICULTY	Average	4	of possible	10
OVERALL CONDITION	Average	4	of possible	10
GREENS CONDITION	Good	6	of possible	10
HAZARDS	Good	6	of possible	10
COSMETICS	Below Average	1	of possible	5
TOTAL	**Average**	**45**	**of possible**	**100**

Description This golf course is flat with narrow to wide fairways bordered by young to mature oak, pine, and eucalyptus trees. It is surrounded on one side by residential housing and a river levee on the other side. Trees, bunkers, and lakes provide the hazards. There are a few interesting holes, but this course is very similar to most of the other golf courses in the San Joaquin Valley.

QUALITY RANKING **78th** **VALUE RANKING** **25th**
Clubhouse Facilities **FAIR** Pro shop, snack bar

Practice Facilities **FAIR** Driving range, putting green

Who Should Play Everyone

Walkability Easy

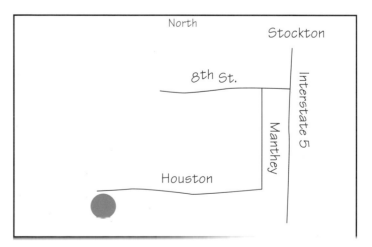

Directions *From downtown Stockton: Go south on Interstate 5. Exit west on 8th Street. Go south on Manthey. Go west on Houston to the golf course.*

Quality Rating	**39**
Value Rating	**C**

SWENSON PARK GOLF COURSE

Address	6803 Alexandria
City, Zip	Stockton, 95207
Telephone	(209) 477–0774
Ownership	Municipal
Weekday Fee	$6.50
Weekend Fee	$7.50
Twilight Fee	$5.50

Men's Par	72
Men's Yardage	6479
Men's Rating	70.1
Women's Par	74
Women's Yardage	6198
Women's Rating	74.0
Championship Yardage	—
Championship Rating	—

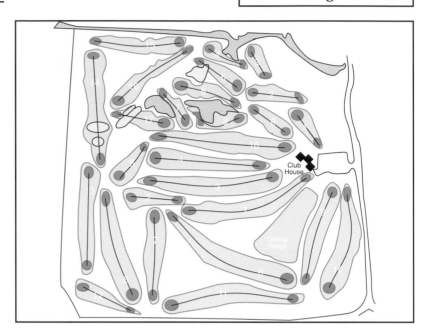

OVERALL APPEAL	Average	6	of possible	15
DESIGN & VARIETY	Average	6	of possible	15
SCENERY	Average	6	of possible	15
OVERALL DIFFICULTY	Good	6	of possible	10
GREENS DIFFICULTY	Average	4	of possible	10
OVERALL CONDITION	Below Average	2	of possible	10
GREENS CONDITION	Average	4	of possible	10
HAZARDS	Average	4	of possible	10
COSMETICS	Below Average	1	of possible	5
TOTAL	**Below Average**	**39**	**of possible**	**100**

Description   This course is flat with medium to wide fairways bordered by middle-aged to mature oak and pine trees. It is surrounded by residential housing. Trees, high-lipped bunkers, and a lake provide the hazards. Most of the holes tend to be straight and without much character.

QUALITY RANKING   90th   VALUE RANKING   68th
Clubhouse Facilities   FAIR   Pro shop, snack bar

Practice Facilities   FAIR   Driving range, 2 putting greens
Who Should Play   Everyone

Walkability   Easy

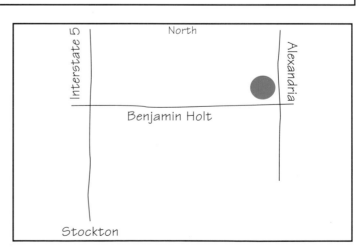

Directions   *From downtown Stockton: Go north on Interstate 5. Exit east on Benjamin Holt and continue about ½ mile. Go north on Alexandria to the golf course.*

132

DRY CREEK GOLF COURSE

Address	809 Crystal Way
City, Zip	Galt, 95632
Telephone	(209) 745–GOLF
Ownership	Independent
Weekday Fee	$11
Weekend Fee	$17
Twilight Fee	—

Men's Par	72
Men's Yardage	6464
Men's Rating	70.8
Women's Par	74
Women's Yardage	5942
Women's Rating	73.4
Championship Yardage	6707
Championship Rating	71.7

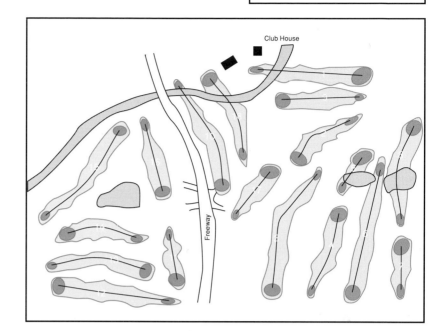

OVERALL APPEAL	Average	6	of possible	15
DESIGN & VARIETY	Very Good	12	of possible	15
SCENERY	Below Average	3	of possible	15
OVERALL DIFFICULTY	Very Good	8	of possible	10
GREENS DIFFICULTY	Good	6	of possible	10
OVERALL CONDITION	Below Average	2	of possible	10
GREENS CONDITION	Average	4	of possible	10
HAZARDS	Very Good	8	of possible	10
COSMETICS	Below Average	1	of possible	5
TOTAL	**Average**	**50**	**of possible**	**100**

Description   This course is flat with a few small hills. The fairways are narrow to medium-wide bordered by mature oak and pine trees. Highway 99 is on one side and the other side is surrounded by open land. Bunkers and many large trees provide most of the hazards. There is some water. It can play difficult with emphasis on accurate driving. It could be a much better golf course to play if cosmetics and maintenance were improved.

QUALITY RANKING   67th   VALUE RANKING   59th

Clubhouse Facilities   GOOD   Pro shop, coffee shop, full bar

Practice Facilities   FAIR   Driving range, putting green

Who Should Play   Everyone

Walkability   Easy

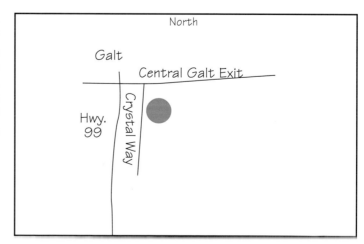

Directions   *From Galt: Go south on Highway 99 and exit east on the Central Galt exit. Go south on Crystal Way to the golf course.*

133

BETHEL ISLAND GOLF COURSE

BETHEL ISLAND GOLF COURSE

Address	3303 Gateway Road
City, Zip	Bethel Island, 94511
Telephone	(415) 684–2654
Ownership	Independent
Weekday Fee	$7
Weekend Fee	$9
Twilight Fee	—

Men's Par	72
Men's Yardage	6120
Men's Rating	68.8
Women's Par	74
Women's Yardage	5713
Women's Rating	71.3
Championship Yardage	6333
Championship Rating	69.4

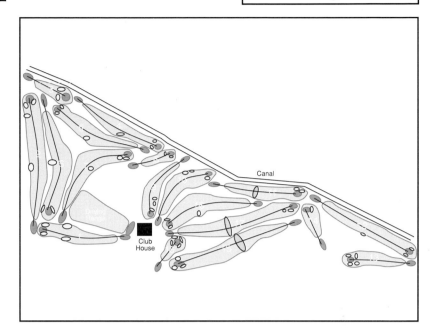

OVERALL APPEAL	Below Average	3	of possible	15
DESIGN & VARIETY	Below Average	3	of possible	15
SCENERY	Below Average	3	of possible	15
OVERALL DIFFICULTY	Average	4	of possible	10
GREENS DIFFICULTY	Below Average	2	of possible	10
OVERALL CONDITION	Average	4	of possible	10
GREENS CONDITION	Average	4	of possible	10
HAZARDS	Below Average	2	of possible	10
COSMETICS	Below Average	1	of possible	5
TOTAL	**Below Average**	**26**	**of possible**	**100**

Description   This course is flat with medium to wide fairways bordered by a few young to middle-aged trees. It is located on Bethel Island in the San Joaquin Delta. Open land surrounds the course. A few bunkers and trees provide the hazards. Most of the holes tend to look the same.

QUALITY RANKING 107th VALUE RANKING 88th

Clubhouse Facilities FAIR Pro shop, snack bar, full bar

Practice Facilities FAIR Driving range, putting green

Who Should Play Those looking for convenience

Walkability Easy

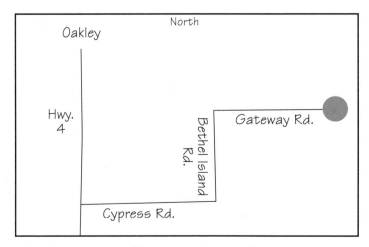

Directions   *From Oakley: Go south on Highway 4. Go east on Cypress Road about 3 miles. Go north on Bethel Island Road about 2 miles. Go east on Gateway Road to the golf course.*

GREEN TREE GOLF COURSE

Address	999 Leisure Town Road
City, Zip	Vacaville, 95688
Telephone	(707) 448–1420
Ownership	Independent
Weekday Fee	$7
Weekend Fee	$10
Twilight Fee	$5.50

Men's Par	71
Men's Yardage	5906
Men's Rating	67.1
Women's Par	71
Women's Yardage	5318
Women's Rating	68.2
Championship Yardage	6370
Championship Rating	69.1

OVERALL APPEAL	Poor	0	of possible	15
DESIGN & VARIETY	Below Average	3	of possible	15
SCENERY	Poor	0	of possible	15
OVERALL DIFFICULTY	Below Average	2	of possible	10
GREENS DIFFICULTY	Below Average	2	of possible	10
OVERALL CONDITION	Poor	0	of possible	10
GREENS CONDITION	Poor	0	of possible	10
HAZARDS	Below Average	2	of possible	10
COSMETICS	Average	2	of possible	5
TOTAL	**Poor**	**11**	**of possible**	**100**

Description This course is flat with medium-wide fairways bordered by middle-aged oak, pine, and eucalyptus trees. It is surrounded by residential housing. Trees, bunkers, and some water provide the hazards. Most of the holes are very boring. Also, negligent maintenance seems to prevail at this course.

QUALITY RANKING 111th   VALUE RANKING 112th
Clubhouse Facilities POOR Pro shop, snack bar

Practice Facilities FAIR Driving range, putting green, chipping green

Who Should Play Those looking for convenience

Walkability Easy

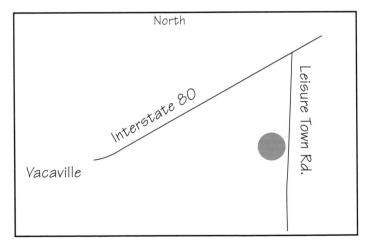

Directions *Go north on Interstate 80 about 2 miles. Exit south on Leisure Town Road to the golf course.*

Quality Rating	**44**
Value Rating	**C**

BING MALONEY GOLF COURSE

Address	6801 Freeport Boulevard
City, Zip	Sacramento, 95822
Telephone	(916) 428–9401
Ownership	Municipal
Weekday Fee	$8.50
Weekend Fee	$9.50
Twilight Fee	$4.25

Men's Par	72
Men's Yardage	6281
Men's Rating	69.7
Women's Par	72
Women's Yardage	5756
Women's Rating	—
Championship Yardage	—
Championship Rating	—

OVERALL APPEAL	Average	6	of possible	15
DESIGN & VARIETY	Average	6	of possible	15
SCENERY	Average	6	of possible	15
OVERALL DIFFICULTY	Average	4	of possible	10
GREENS DIFFICULTY	Good	6	of possible	10
OVERALL CONDITION	Average	4	of possible	10
GREENS CONDITION	Good	6	of possible	10
HAZARDS	Good	6	of possible	10
COSMETICS	Poor	0	of possible	5
TOTAL	**Average**	**44**	**of possible**	**100**

Description This golf course is flat with medium to wide fairways bordered by middle-aged to mature pine and oak trees. It has residential housing on one side and the Sacramento Executive Airport on the other side. Trees and deep bunkers provide the hazards. There is some water. This course is pretty standard for the San Joaquin Valley. However, the greens are quite large and deep bunkers are placed so there can be easy or difficult pin placements.

QUALITY RANKING 80th VALUE RANKING 49th

Clubhouse Facilities FAIR Pro shop, snack bar

Practice Facilities GOOD Driving range, putting green

Who Should Play Everyone

Walkability Easy

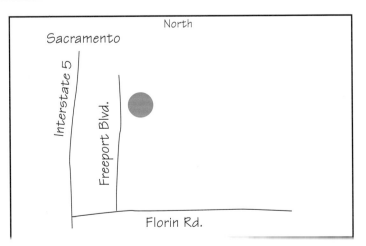

Directions *From downtown Sacramento: Go south on Interstate 5. Exit east on Florin Road. Go North on Freeport Boulevard to the golf course.*

HAGGIN OAKS GOLF COURSE —SOUTH

Address	3645 Fulton Avenue
City, Zip	Sacramento, 95821
Telephone	(916) 481–4506
Ownership	Municipal
Weekday Fee	$8.50
Weekend Fee	$9.50
Twilight Fee	$4.25

Men's Par	72
Men's Yardage	6216
Men's Rating	69.1
Women's Par	72
Women's Yardage	5592
Women's Rating	71.6
Championship Yardage	—
Championship Rating	—

OVERALL APPEAL	Good	9	of possible	15
DESIGN & VARIETY	Good	9	of possible	15
SCENERY	Good	9	of possible	15
OVERALL DIFFICULTY	Good	6	of possible	10
GREENS DIFFICULTY	Average	4	of possible	10
OVERALL CONDITION	Average	4	of possible	10
GREENS CONDITION	Average	4	of possible	10
HAZARDS	Good	6	of possible	10
COSMETICS	Average	2	of possible	5
TOTAL	**Average**	**53**	**of possible**	**100**

Description This golf course is flat with narrow to medium-wide fairways bordered by mature oak and pine trees. Highway 80 is on one side and railroad tracks are on the other side. Trees, bunkers, and some water provide the hazards. Many of the holes look the same. However, the challenge of the golf course and the mature trees make this a fun course to play. It could be a good course if the maintenance was improved. 9th BEST PRACTICE FACILITIES

QUALITY RANKING 56th   VALUE RANKING   31st
Clubhouse Facilities   FAIR Pro shop, snack bar

Practice Facilities   EXCELLENT Driving range, 2 putting greens, chipping green
Who Should Play Everyone

Walkability Easy

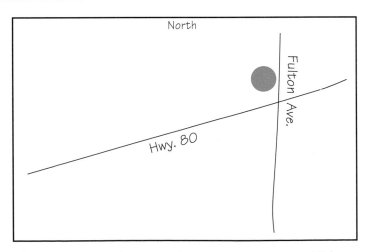

Directions From downtown Sacramento: Go east on Highway 80. Exit north on Fulton Avenue to the golf course.

| Poor | Below Average | Average | Good | Very Good | Outstanding |

Quality Rating	**31**
Value Rating	**D**

HAGGIN OAKS GOLF COURSE
—RED/BLUE

Address	3645 Fulton Avenue
City, Zip	Sacramento, 95821
Telephone	(916) 481–4508
Ownership	Municipal
Weekday Fee	$8.50
Weekend Fee	$9.50
Twilight Fee	—

Men's Par	72
Men's Yardage	6547
Men's Rating	70.4
Women's Par	72
Women's Yardage	5834
Women's Rating	72.0
Championship Yardage	6860
Championship Rating	72.0

OVERALL APPEAL	Below Average	3	of possible	15
DESIGN & VARIETY	Below Average	3	of possible	15
SCENERY	Average	6	of possible	15
OVERALL DIFFICULTY	Very Good	8	of possible	10
GREENS DIFFICULTY	Average	4	of possible	10
OVERALL CONDITION	Below Average	2	of possible	10
GREENS CONDITION	Below Average	2	of possible	10
HAZARDS	Below Average	2	of possible	10
COSMETICS	Below Average	1	of possible	5
TOTAL	**Below Average**	**31**	**of possible**	**100**

Description   This golf course is flat with medium to wide fairways bordered by young to middle-aged oak trees. Highway 80 borders this course. A few bunkers and scattered trees provide the hazards. Almost all the holes look the same. The course is boring to play with most of the holes being straight. There is one good par 5 that cuts across a creek. 9th BEST PRACTICE FACILITIES

QUALITY RANKING   98th   VALUE RANKING   90th
Clubhouse Facilities   FAIR   Pro shop, snack bar

Practice Facilities   EXCELLENT   Driving range, 2 putting greens, chipping green
Who Should Play   Everyone

Walkability   Easy

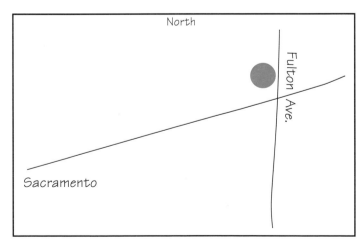

Directions   *From downtown Sacramento: Go east on Highway 80. Exit north on Fulton Avenue to the golf course.*

Poor	Below Average	Average	Good	Very Good	Outstanding

Quality Rating	33
Value Rating	F

RIVERBEND GOLF & COUNTRY CLUB

Address	500 Douglas Street
City, Zip	West Sacramento, 95605
Telephone	(916) 372–0810
Ownership	Independent
Weekday Fee	$13
Weekend Fee	$15
Twilight Fee	—

Men's Par	70
Men's Yardage	5521
Men's Rating	64.8
Women's Par	70
Women's Yardage	5216
Women's Rating	69.0
Championship Yardage	—
Championship Rating	—

OVERALL APPEAL	Below Average	3	of possible	15
DESIGN & VARIETY	Poor	0	of possible	15
SCENERY	Average	6	of possible	15
OVERALL DIFFICULTY	Below Average	2	of possible	10
GREENS DIFFICULTY	Below Average	2	of possible	10
OVERALL CONDITION	Good	6	of possible	10
GREENS CONDITION	Good	6	of possible	10
HAZARDS	Good	6	of possible	10
COSMETICS	Average	2	of possible	5
TOTAL	**Below Average**	**33**	**of possible**	**100**

Description This golf course is flat with very narrow fairways bordered by middle-aged to mature pine and oak trees. It is located near a residential area. Trees, bunkers, and some water provide the hazards. It is a short course with many of the holes looking the same. The average par 4 is just over 300 yards. Management does take pride in their facilities.

QUALITY RANKING   95th   VALUE RANKING   103rd
Clubhouse Facilities   FAIR   Pro shop, snack bar, banquet
Practice Facilities   FAIR   Driving range, 2 putting greens
Who Should Play   Beginners

Walkability   Easy

Directions   *In West Sacramento from Highway 80: Exit north on Jefferson Boulevard. Go east on Sacramento Avenue. Go north on Douglas Street to the golf course.*

140

Poor	Below Average	Average	Good	Very Good	Outstanding
☐	☐	☐	■	☐	☐

Quality Rating 67

Value Rating A

ANCIL HOFFMAN GOLF COURSE

Address	6700 Tarshes Drive
City, Zip	Carmichael, 95608
Telephone	(916) 482–5660
Ownership	County
Weekday Fee	$9.50
Weekend Fee	$11
Twilight Fee	$7

Men's Par	72
Men's Yardage	6434
Men's Rating	70.2
Women's Par	73
Women's Yardage	5954
Women's Rating	73.3
Championship Yardage	6794
Championship Rating	71.9

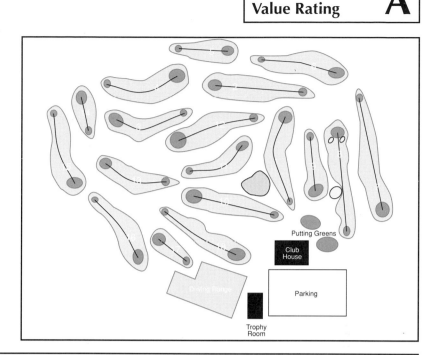

OVERALL APPEAL	Good	9	of possible	15
DESIGN & VARIETY	Very Good	12	of possible	15
SCENERY	Good	9	of possible	15
OVERALL DIFFICULTY	Very Good	8	of possible	10
GREENS DIFFICULTY	Good	6	of possible	10
OVERALL CONDITION	Good	6	of possible	10
GREENS CONDITION	Good	6	of possible	10
HAZARDS	Very Good	8	of possible	10
COSMETICS	Good	3	of possible	5
TOTAL	**Good**	**67**	**of possible**	**100**

Description   This course is flat with a few undulations in the fairways. Fairways are narrow to medium-wide bordered by mature oak and pine trees. The American River borders one side of the course and the other side is adjacent to Ancil Hoffman Park. Trees, well-placed bunkers, and some water provide the hazards. It is a challenging course with many nice doglegs. Emphasis is on accuracy off the tee.

QUALITY RANKING   37th   VALUE RANKING   8th

Clubhouse Facilities   FAIR   Pro shop, snack bar

Practice Facilities   GOOD   Driving range, 2 putting greens

Who Should Play   Those looking for a challenge

Walkability   Easy

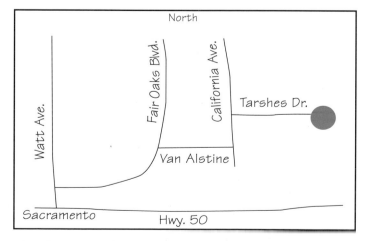

Directions   *From downtown Sacramento: Go east on Highway 50. Go north on Watt Avenue. Go east on Fair Oaks Boulevard. Go east on Van Alstine Avenue. Go north on California Avenue. Go east on Tarshes Drive to the golf course.*

141

DIAMOND OAKS MUNICIPAL GOLF COURSE

☐	☐	■	☐	☐	☐
Poor	Below Average	Average	Good	Very Good	Outstanding

Quality Rating 57

Value Rating B

DIAMOND OAKS MUNICIPAL GOLF COURSE

Address	349 Diamond Oaks Boulevard
City, Zip	Roseville, 95661
Telephone	(916) 783–4947
Ownership	Municipal
Weekday Fee	$6.50
Weekend Fee	$7.50
Twilight Fee	$3.75

Men's Par	72
Men's Yardage	6065
Men's Rating	69.0
Women's Par	73
Women's Yardage	5456
Women's Rating	68.9
Championship Yardage	6283
Championship Rating	—

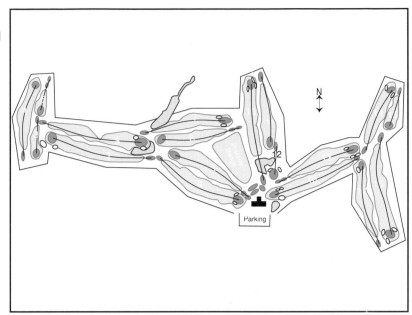

OVERALL APPEAL	Good	9	of possible	15
DESIGN & VARIETY	Good	9	of possible	15
SCENERY	Good	9	of possible	15
OVERALL DIFFICULTY	Average	4	of possible	10
GREENS DIFFICULTY	Good	6	of possible	10
OVERALL CONDITION	Good	6	of possible	10
GREENS CONDITION	Good	6	of possible	10
HAZARDS	Good	6	of possible	10
COSMETICS	Average	2	of possible	5
TOTAL	**Average**	**57**	**of possible**	**100**

Description   This course has rolling hills with narrow to wide fairways bordered by mature oak trees. Residential housing is on one side and open land is on the other side. Trees, bunkers, and water provide the hazards. It is an enjoyable course to play with lots of fun holes. It has a few more hills than your other San Joaquin Valley courses. Management takes pride in their facilities.

QUALITY RANKING   49th   VALUE RANKING   12th

Clubhouse Facilities   FAIR   Pro shop, snack bar

Practice Facilities   FAIR   Driving range, putting green

Who Should Play   Everyone

Walkability   Moderate

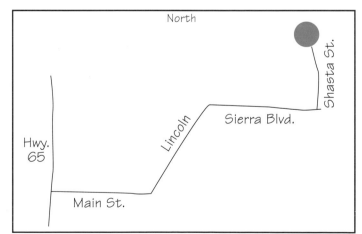

Directions   *Go north on Highway 65. In downtown Roseville go east on Main Street. Go north on Lincoln (it turns into Sierra Boulevard). Go north on Shasta Street to the golf course.*

143

Poor	Below Average	Average	Good	Very Good	Outstanding
☐	☐	■	☐	☐	☐

Quality Rating 52

Value Rating C

PLUMAS LAKE GOLF & COUNTRY CLUB

Address	1551 Country Club Avenue
City, Zip	Marysville, 95901
Telephone	(916) 742–3201
Ownership	Independent
Weekday Fee	$12
Weekend Fee	$15
Twilight Fee	$6

Men's Par	71
Men's Yardage	6153
Men's Rating	68.7
Women's Par	72
Women's Yardage	5759
Women's Rating	72.3
Championship Yardage	—
Championship Rating	69.9

OVERALL APPEAL	Average	6	of possible	15
DESIGN & VARIETY	Average	6	of possible	15
SCENERY	Average	6	of possible	15
OVERALL DIFFICULTY	Good	6	of possible	10
GREENS DIFFICULTY	Good	6	of possible	10
OVERALL CONDITION	Very Good	8	of possible	10
GREENS CONDITION	Good	6	of possible	10
HAZARDS	Good	6	of possible	10
COSMETICS	Average	2	of possible	5
TOTAL	**Average**	**52**	**of possible**	**100**

Description This course is flat with a few small hills. Fairways are medium to wide and bordered by middle-aged to mature oak, pine, and eucalyptus trees. It is surrounded by open land. Trees, bunkers, and a drainage ditch provide the hazards. Most of the holes tend to look the same. There are many side-by-side fairways. However, a drainage ditch winds around the course creating a few interesting holes. Management takes pride in maintaining their facilities.

QUALITY RANKING 60th VALUE RANKING 63rd

Clubhouse Facilities   FAIR   Pro shop, snack bar, full bar

Practice Facilities   FAIR   Driving range, 2 putting greens

Who Should Play   Everyone

Walkability   Moderate

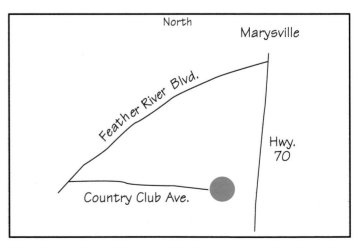

Directions   *From Highway 70: Exit south on Feather River Boulevard about 6 miles. Go east on Country Club Avenue to the golf course.*

144

Poor	Below Average	Average	Good	Very Good	Outstanding
☐	■	☐	☐	☐	☐

Quality Rating	**29**
Value Rating	**D**

TABLE MOUNTAIN GOLF COURSE

Address	P.O. Box 2769
City, Zip	Oroville, 95965
Telephone	(916) 533–3922
Ownership	Independent
Weekday Fee	$8
Weekend Fee	$10
Twilight Fee	$5.50

Men's Par	72
Men's Yardage	6472
Men's Rating	70.1
Women's Par	72
Women's Yardage	5882
Women's Rating	72.8
Championship Yardage	—
Championship Rating	—

OVERALL APPEAL	Below Average	3	of possible	15
DESIGN & VARIETY	Below Average	3	of possible	15
SCENERY	Poor	0	of possible	15
OVERALL DIFFICULTY	Good	6	of possible	10
GREENS DIFFICULTY	Average	4	of possible	10
OVERALL CONDITION	Below Average	2	of possible	10
GREENS CONDITION	Good	6	of possible	10
HAZARDS	Average	4	of possible	10
COSMETICS	Below Average	1	of possible	5
TOTAL	**Below Average**	**29**	**of possible**	**100**

Description   This course is flat with medium-wide fairways bordered by young to middle-aged eucalyptus and pine trees. It is surrounded by open land. Trees, bunkers, and some water provide the hazards. Almost every hole looks the same, making this course boring to play. Water provides a few interesting holes.

QUALITY RANKING 102nd   VALUE RANKING 92nd

Clubhouse Facilities   FAIR   Pro shop, snack bar, full bar

Practice Facilities   FAIR   Matted driving range, putting green, chipping green, bunker

Who Should Play   Those looking for convenience

Walkability   Easy

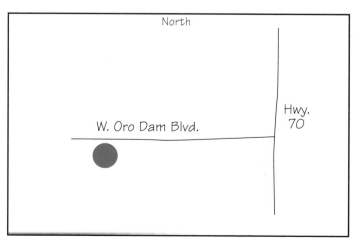

Directions   *From Highway 70: Exit west on W. Oro Dam Boulevard about 2 miles to the golf course.*

☐	☐	■	☐	☐	☐
Poor	Below Average	Average	Good	Very Good	Outstanding

BIDWELL PARK GOLF COURSE

Address	P.O. Box 501
City, Zip	Chico, 95927
Telephone	(916) 891–8417
Ownership	Municipal
Weekday Fee	$8.50
Weekend Fee	$11
Twilight Fee	$6

Men's Par	70
Men's Yardage	6163
Men's Rating	68.1
Women's Par	70
Women's Yardage	5780
Women's Rating	72.0
Championship Yardage	—
Championship Rating	—

OVERALL APPEAL	Good	9	of possible	15
DESIGN & VARIETY	Good	9	of possible	15
SCENERY	Good	9	of possible	15
OVERALL DIFFICULTY	Average	4	of possible	10
GREENS DIFFICULTY	Good	6	of possible	10
OVERALL CONDITION	Average	4	of possible	10
GREENS CONDITION	Average	4	of possible	10
HAZARDS	Good	6	of possible	10
COSMETICS	Average	2	of possible	5
TOTAL	**Average**	**53**	**of possible**	**100**

Description This course is flat with a few small hills. It has a parklike setting. Fairways are narrow to wide and bordered by a variety of mature trees. Trees, bunkers, and some water provide the hazards. The course has an interesting design with no difficult holes making it a fun course to play. There are beautiful trees with many greens nicely tucked behind them.

QUALITY RANKING 59th   VALUE RANKING 32nd
Clubhouse Facilities FAIR Pro shop, snack bar

Practice Facilities FAIR Driving range, 2 putting greens

Who Should Play Everyone

Walkability Moderate

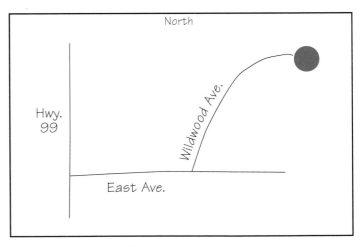

Directions *From Highway 99: Exit east on East Avenue about 4 miles. Go north on Wildwood Avenue about 1½ miles to the golf course.*

| Poor | Below Average | Average | Good | Very Good | Outstanding |

| Quality Rating | **63** |
| Value Rating | **C** |

WILCOX OAKS GOLF CLUB

Address   P.O. Box 127
City, Zip   Red Bluff, 96080
Telephone   (916) 527–7087
Ownership   Independent
Weekday Fee $15
Weekend Fee $20
Twilight Fee   —

Men's Par   72
Men's Yardage   6101
Men's Rating   68.4
Women's Par   72
Women's Yardage   5779
Women's Rating   71.5
Championship
    Yardage   —
Championship
    Rating   —

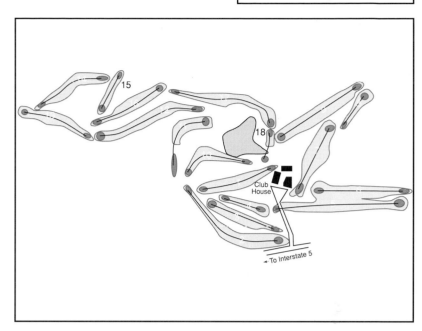

OVERALL APPEAL	Very Good	12	of possible	15
DESIGN & VARIETY	Very Good	12	of possible	15
SCENERY	Very Good	12	of possible	15
OVERALL DIFFICULTY	Good	6	of possible	10
GREENS DIFFICULTY	Good	6	of possible	10
OVERALL CONDITION	Average	4	of possible	10
GREENS CONDITION	Average	4	of possible	10
HAZARDS	Good	6	of possible	10
COSMETICS	Below Average	1	of possible	5
TOTAL	**Good**	**63**	**of possible**	**100**

Description   This course has rolling hills with narrow to medium-wide fairways bordered by middle-aged to mature oak trees. It is located in the foothills in a solid, oak-tree forest. Trees, bunkers, and some water provide the hazards. The holes seem to meander through the hills with very few side-by-side fairways. Emphasis is on accuracy off the tee. Many interesting holes make for an enjoyable round of golf.

QUALITY RANKING 44th   VALUE RANKING 40th
Clubhouse Facilities FAIR Pro shop (other clubhouse facilities are closed to the public)
Practice Facilities FAIR Matted driving range, 2 putting greens
Who Should Play Everyone

Walkability Moderate

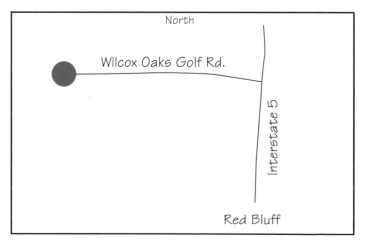

Directions   *Go north on Interstate 5 about 3 miles. Exit west on Wilcox Oaks Golf Road to the golf course.*

GOLD HILLS GOLF CLUB

Poor	Below Average	Average	Good	Very Good	Outstanding

Quality Rating	**59**
Value Rating	**C**

GOLD HILLS GOLF CLUB

Address	2101 Gold Hill Drive
City, Zip	Redding, 96003
Telephone	(916) 246–7867
Ownership	Independent
Weekday Fee	$12
Weekend Fee	$14
Twilight Fee	—

Men's Par	72
Men's Yardage	6186
Men's Rating	69.5
Women's Par	72
Women's Yardage	5561
Women's Rating	71.2
Championship Yardage	6624
Championship Rating	71.5

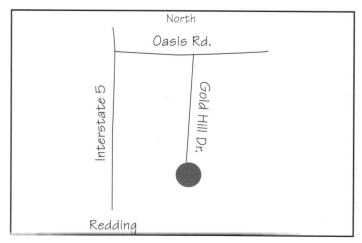

OVERALL APPEAL	Average	6	of possible	15
DESIGN & VARIETY	Very Good	12	of possible	15
SCENERY	Very Good	12	of possible	15
OVERALL DIFFICULTY	Very Good	8	of possible	10
GREENS DIFFICULTY	Good	6	of possible	10
OVERALL CONDITION	Poor	0	of possible	10
GREENS CONDITION	Average	4	of possible	10
HAZARDS	Outstanding	10	of possible	10
COSMETICS	Below Average	1	of possible	5
TOTAL	**Average**	**59**	**of possible**	**100**

Description This course is hilly with narrow to wide fairways bordered by middle-aged to mature oak trees. It is located in the foothills with residential housing surrounding many of the fairways. Trees, many creeks, and water provide ample hazards. The course is exciting to play with a wide variety of holes ranging from flat to quite hilly. Unfortunately, an almost entire lack of maintenance has created a "pasturelike" appearance. With proper maintenance it could be a much better golf course.

QUALITY RANKING 48th VALUE RANKING 54th
Clubhouse Facilities GOOD Pro shop, coffee shop, full bar
Practice Facilities GOOD Driving range, putting green, chipping green, bunker
Who Should Play Everyone

Walkability Difficult

Directions *Go north on Interstate 5. Exit east on Oasis Road. Go south on Gold Hill Drive to the golf course.*

149

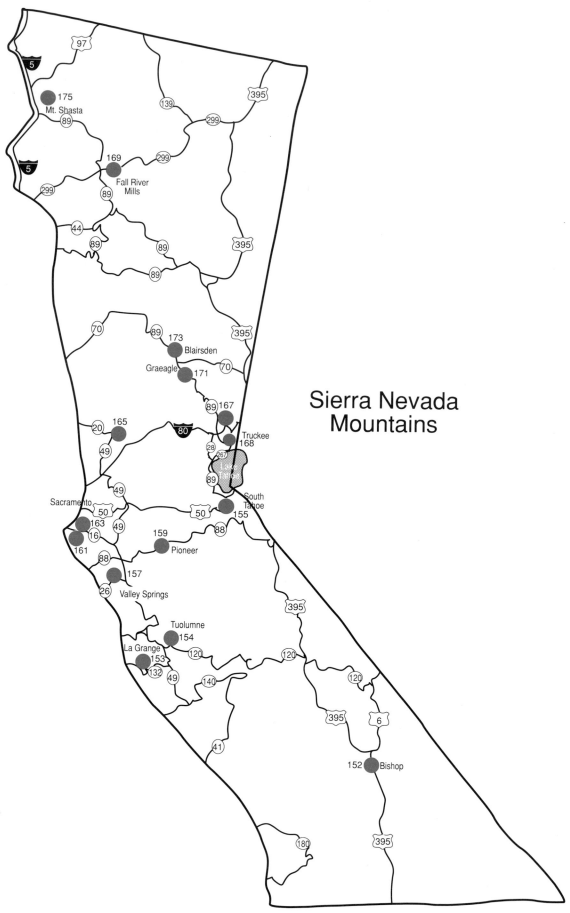

Sierra Nevada Mountains

Numbered dots indicate the page number where the golf course is described.

SIERRA NEVADA MOUNTAINS

The Sierra Nevada Mountains offer golf courses with beautiful scenery. This zone covers an area from the foothills in the west to the Nevada/California stateline in the east and from Sequoia National Park in the south to the Oregon/California stateline in the north.

Some of the courses are set in rolling foothills with beautiful, mature oak trees and panoramic views. Others are higher up in elevation in magnificent pine forests. A few of these courses are located in popular resort areas while others are in very remote locations.

Weather conditions vary a great deal from season to season. Wintertime will close most of the courses in the higher elevations as they get covered with snow. Courses in the foothills stay open on a year-round basis. In the summer, beautiful weather allows for very pleasant outings on the golf course. Playing golf in the fall at some courses is most scenic, with leaves changing colors on the trees. Remember, always bring a sweater and wind-breaker as the weather can be very unpredictable.

There are no municipal/county 18-hole golf courses in the Sierra Nevada Mountain zone.

Most independent courses are moderately priced. Dress codes ranges from informal to formal golf attire. Maintenance conditions range from poor to very good. Most of the courses are busy on weekends in high season and pretty much open on weekdays.

The resort golf courses are expensive. However, most offer golf packages to reduce your cost. They tend to be upscale and golf attire is formal. Good to outstanding quality is offered at these courses.

Poor	Below Average	Average	Good	Very Good	Outstanding
☐	☐	■	☐	☐	☐

Quality Rating	**47**
Value Rating	**C**

BISHOP COUNTRY CLUB

Address	P.O. Box 1586
City, Zip	Bishop, 93514
Telephone	(619) 873–5828
Ownership	Independent
Weekday Fee	$14
Weekend Fee	$16
Twilight Fee	—

Men's Par	71
Men's Yardage	6072
Men's Rating	67.3
Women's Par	71
Women's Yardage	5467
Women's Rating	70.3
Championship Yardage	6613
Championship Rating	69.3

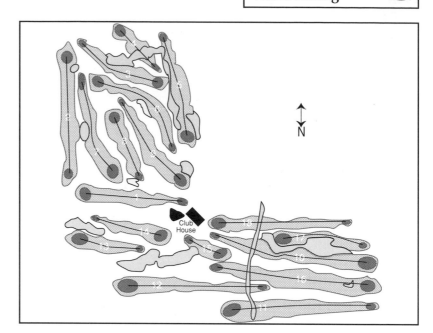

OVERALL APPEAL	Average	6	of possible	15
DESIGN & VARIETY	Average	6	of possible	15
SCENERY	Good	9	of possible	15
OVERALL DIFFICULTY	Average	4	of possible	10
GREENS DIFFICULTY	Good	6	of possible	10
OVERALL CONDITION	Average	4	of possible	10
GREENS CONDITION	Good	6	of possible	10
HAZARDS	Average	4	of possible	10
COSMETICS	Average	2	of possible	5
TOTAL	**Average**	**47**	**of possible**	**100**

Description This course is flat with medium to wide fairways bordered by young to mature trees. Open land surrounds it with distant views of the Sierra Nevada Mountains. Trees, bunkers, and plenty of water provide the hazards. Most of the holes tend to look the same. With water hazards there are a few interesting holes to play.

QUALITY RANKING 74th   VALUE RANKING 79th
Clubhouse Facilities FAIR Pro shop, coffee shop, full bar
Practice Facilities FAIR Driving range, putting green, bunker
Who Should Play Everyone

Walkability Easy

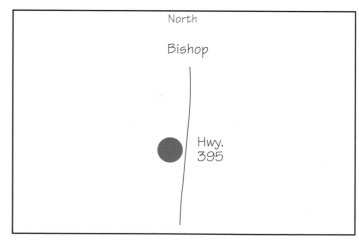

Directions *Go south on Highway 395 about 1½ miles to the golf course.*

LAKE DON PEDRO GOLF & COUNTRY CLUB

Address	P.O. Box 193
City, Zip	La Grange, 95329
Telephone	(209) 852–2242
Ownership	Independent
Weekday Fee	$8
Weekend Fee	$10
Twilight Fee	—

Men's Par	70
Men's Yardage	6007
Men's Rating	67.4
Women's Par	72
Women's Yardage	5561
Women's Rating	70.7
Championship Yardage	6244
Championship Rating	68.6

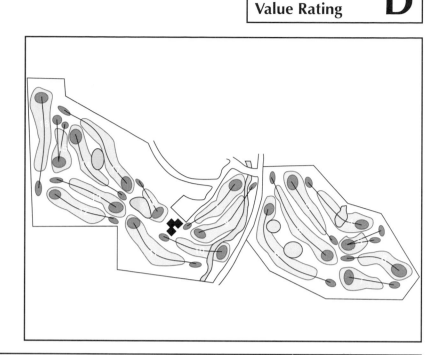

OVERALL APPEAL	Poor	0	of possible	15
DESIGN & VARIETY	Average	6	of possible	15
SCENERY	Good	9	of possible	15
OVERALL DIFFICULTY	Average	4	of possible	10
GREENS DIFFICULTY	Average	4	of possible	10
OVERALL CONDITION	Poor	0	of possible	10
GREENS CONDITION	Poor	0	of possible	10
HAZARDS	Average	4	of possible	10
COSMETICS	Poor	0	of possible	5
TOTAL	**Below Average**	**27**	**of possible**	**100**

Description   This course has rolling hills with medium to wide fairways bordered by middle-aged oak trees. It is located in the foothills with some housing bordering the course. Trees, bunkers, and some water provide the hazards. It is a short course with lots of interesting holes. However, negligent maintenance ruins the appeal of this course. With proper maintenance it could be a good one.

QUALITY RANKING 104th   VALUE RANKING 96th

Clubhouse Facilities   GOOD   Pro shop, coffee shop, full bar

Practice Facilities   POOR   Putting green

Who Should Play   Those looking for convenience

Walkability   Difficult

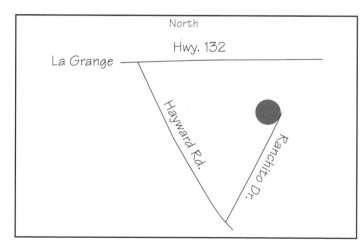

Directions   *Go east on Highway 132 about 2 miles. Go south on Hayward Road about 2 miles. Go north on Ranchito Drive to the golf course.*

Poor	Below Average	Average	Good ■	Very Good	Outstanding

PINE MOUNTAIN LAKE COUNTRY CLUB

Address	P.O. Box P.M.L.A.
City, Zip	Groveland, 95321
Telephone	(209) 962–7471
Ownership	Resort
Weekday Fee	$20
Weekend Fee	$20
Twilight Fee	—

Men's Par	70
Men's Yardage	6106
Men's Rating	68.4
Women's Par	71
Women's Yardage	5701
Women's Rating	72
Championship Yardage	6351
Championship Rating	69.4

OVERALL APPEAL	Very Good	12	of possible	15
DESIGN & VARIETY	Very Good	12	of possible	15
SCENERY	Outstanding	15	of possible	15
OVERALL DIFFICULTY	Very Good	8	of possible	10
GREENS DIFFICULTY	Very Good	8	of possible	10
OVERALL CONDITION	Good	6	of possible	10
GREENS CONDITION	Good	6	of possible	10
HAZARDS	Good	6	of possible	10
COSMETICS	Good	3	of possible	5
TOTAL	**Good**	**76**	**of possible**	**100**

Description   This course is hilly with narrow to medium-wide fairways bordered by mature oak and pine trees. It is located in a valley near the 2,800-foot elevation. Residential housing borders the fairways. Trees, bunkers, and some water provide the hazards. It's a fun course to play for all levels of golfers. It has a country club atmosphere.

QUALITY RANKING   24th   VALUE RANKING   52nd
Clubhouse Facilities   GOOD   Pro shop, coffee shop, full bar, fine dining
Practice Facilities   FAIR   Driving range, putting green

Who Should Play   Everyone

Walkability   Difficult

Directions   *Go north on Ferratti Road and follow signs to the golf course.*

North

Ferratti Rd.

Hwy. 120   Groveland

Poor Below Average Average **Good** Very Good Outstanding

LAKE TAHOE COUNTRY CLUB

Address	P.O. Box 10406
City, Zip	South Lake Tahoe
Telephone	(916) 577–0788
Ownership	Independent
Weekday Fee	$23
Weekend Fee	$23
Twilight Fee	$15

Men's Par	71
Men's Yardage	6169
Men's Rating	68.2
Women's Par	72
Women's Yardage	5687
Women's Rating	71.5
Championship Yardage	6707
Championship Rating	71.0

OVERALL APPEAL	Very Good	12	of possible	15
DESIGN & VARIETY	Good	9	of possible	15
SCENERY	Outstanding	15	of possible	15
OVERALL DIFFICULTY	Good	6	of possible	10
GREENS DIFFICULTY	Good	6	of possible	10
OVERALL CONDITION	Good	6	of possible	10
GREENS CONDITION	Good	6	of possible	10
HAZARDS	Good	6	of possible	10
COSMETICS	Good	3	of possible	5
TOTAL	**Good**	**69**	**of possible**	**100**

Description   This course is flat with a few small hills. Fairways are medium to wide bordered by mature pine trees. The course is located in the Lake Tahoe Valley with residential housing and open land surrounding it. Trees, bunkers, streams, and lakes provide the hazards. Beautiful scenery and interesting holes make for an enjoyable round of golf. Some holes are out in the open with nice, panoramic views and other holes are cut out of the forest.

QUALITY RANKING   36th   VALUE RANKING   70th

Clubhouse Facilities   FAIR   Pro shop, snack bar, full bar, outside bar-b-q area

Practice Facilities   FAIR   Driving range, putting green

Who Should Play   Everyone

Walkability   Easy

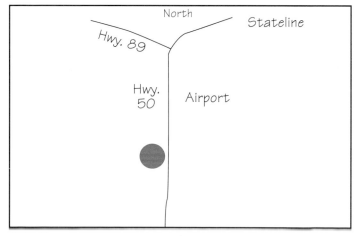

Directions   *From the South Lake Tahoe Airport: Go south on Highway 50 about 1 mile to the golf course.*

155

LA CONTENTA GOLF & COUNTRY CLUB

						Quality Rating	**63**
□ Poor	□ Below Average	□ Average	■ Good	□ Very Good	□ Outstanding	Value Rating	**B**

LA CONTENTA GOLF & COUNTRY CLUB

Address	Route 1, 1653 Highway 26
City, Zip	Valley Springs, 95252
Telephone	(209) 772–1081
Ownership	Independent
Weekday Fee	$10
Weekend Fee	$19
Twilight Fee	$6

Men's Par	72
Men's Yardage	6006
Men's Rating	68.5
Women's Par	73
Women's Yardage	5357
Women's Rating	69.3
Championship Yardage	6421
Championship Rating	70.6

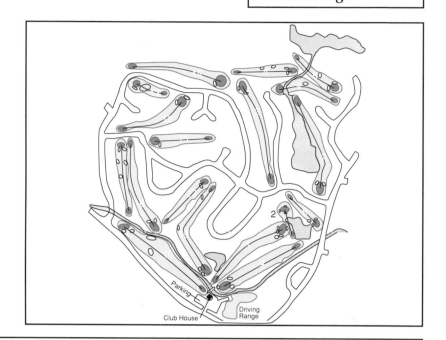

OVERALL APPEAL	Good	9	of possible	15
DESIGN & VARIETY	Very Good	12	of possible	15
SCENERY	Very Good	12	of possible	15
OVERALL DIFFICULTY	Good	6	of possible	10
GREENS DIFFICULTY	Good	6	of possible	10
OVERALL CONDITION	Average	4	of possible	10
GREENS CONDITION	Average	4	of possible	10
HAZARDS	Very Good	8	of possible	10
COSMETICS	Average	2	of possible	5
TOTAL	**Good**	**63**	**of possible**	**100**

Description This course is hilly with narrow to wide fairways bordered by mature oak trees. It is located in the foothills and weaves through residential housing. Trees, hills, bunkers, and strategically placed lakes provide the hazards. It is a fun course with many interesting holes, and very challenging for a shorter course. There are nice views of the surrounding foothills. With improved maintenance and cosmetics it could be a very good course to play.

QUALITY RANKING 42nd VALUE RANKING 16th
Clubhouse Facilities GOOD Pro shop, coffee shop

Practice Facilities FAIR Driving range, putting green

Who Should Play Everyone

Walkability Difficult

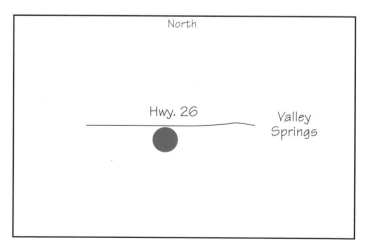

Directions *From Valley Springs: Go west on Highway 26 about ½ mile to the golf course.*

MACE MEADOWS GOLF & COUNTRY
CLUB

☐ Poor	☐ Below Average	☐ Average	■ Good	☐ Very Good	☐ Outstanding

MACE MEADOWS GOLF & COUNTRY CLUB

Address	P.O. Box 502, Highway 88
City, Zip	Pioneer, 95666
Telephone	(209) 295–7020
Ownership	Independent
Weekday Fee	$10
Weekend Fee	$15
Twilight Fee	—

Men's Par	72
Men's Yardage	6602
Men's Rating	70.8
Women's Par	72
Women's Yardage	5666
Women's Rating	72
Championship Yardage	—
Championship Rating	—

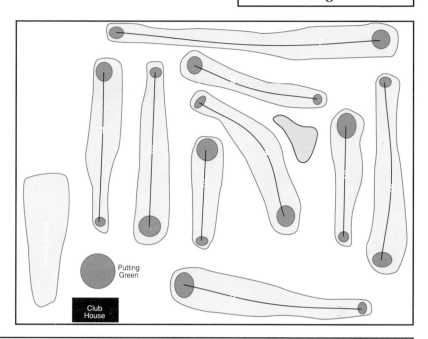

OVERALL APPEAL	Very Good	12	of possible	15
DESIGN & VARIETY	Good	9	of possible	15
SCENERY	Outstanding	15	of possible	15
OVERALL DIFFICULTY	Good	6	of possible	10
GREENS DIFFICULTY	Good	6	of possible	10
OVERALL CONDITION	Good	6	of possible	10
GREENS CONDITION	Very Good	8	of possible	10
HAZARDS	Good	6	of possible	10
COSMETICS	Average	2	of possible	5
TOTAL	**Good**	**70**	**of possible**	**100**

Description This course is flat with a few hills. Fairways are narrow to medium-wide bordered by mature oak and pine trees. The course sits in a beautiful valley near the 3,100-foot elevation. Some residential housing surrounds it. Trees, bunkers, and water provide the hazards. Interesting holes, a good challenge, and beautiful scenery make for a most enjoyable round of golf. (At the time of this rating it was a 9-hole course with an additional 9 holes already constructed and under seeding.)

QUALITY RANKING 34th   VALUE RANKING   9th

Clubhouse Facilities   FAIR   Pro shop, coffee shop

Practice Facilities   FAIR   Driving range, putting green

Who Should Play   Everyone

Walkability   Moderate

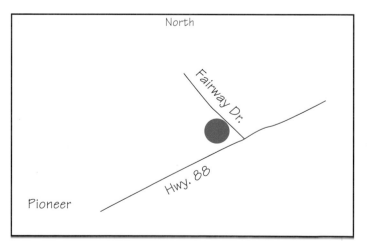

Directions   *In Pioneer: Go east on Highway 88. Go west on Fairway Drive to the golf course.*

RANCHO MURIETA COUNTRY CLUB—SOUTH

Quality Rating	**80**
Value Rating	**D**

RANCHO MURIETA COUNTRY CLUB—SOUTH

Address	14813 Jackson Road
City, Zip	Rancho Murieta, 95683
Telephone	(916) 985–7200
Ownership	Resort
Weekday Fee	$55
Weekend Fee	$55
Twilight Fee	—

Men's Par	72
Men's Yardage	6307
Men's Rating	70.2
Women's Par	72
Women's Yardage	5527
Women's Rating	71.5
Championship Yardage	6886
Championship Rating	72.6

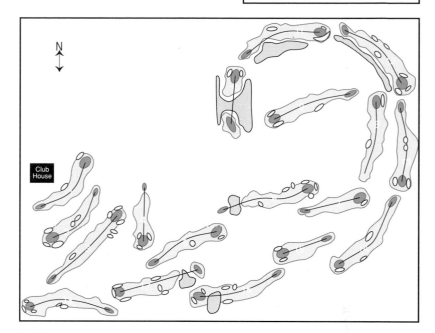

OVERALL APPEAL	Outstanding	15	of possible	15
DESIGN & VARIETY	Outstanding	15	of possible	15
SCENERY	Good	9	of possible	15
OVERALL DIFFICULTY	Outstanding	10	of possible	10
GREENS DIFFICULTY	Good	6	of possible	10
OVERALL CONDITION	Good	6	of possible	10
GREENS CONDITION	Very Good	8	of possible	10
HAZARDS	Very Good	8	of possible	10
COSMETICS	Good	3	of possible	5
TOTAL	**Very Good**	**80**	**of possible**	**100**

Description This course has rolling hills with medium-wide fairways bordered by young to mature oak trees. It is located in the lower foothills with open land surrounding the course. Trees, many bunkers, and water provide the hazards. It's a beautifully designed course that's challenging and very fun to play. There are some nice panoramic views of the surrounding foothills. A country club atmosphere prevails. 4th BEST CLUBHOUSE 10th BEST "FUN COURSE"

QUALITY RANKING 20th   VALUE RANKING 91st

Clubhouse Facilities EXCELLENT Pro shop, snack bar, full bar, fine dining, banquet

Practice Facilities EXCELLENT Driving range, putting green, chipping green, bunkers

Who Should Play Everyone

Walkability Carts are mandatory

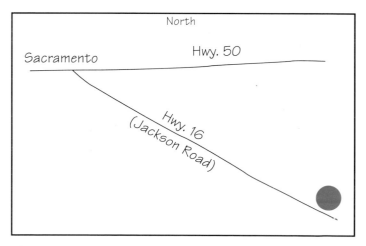

Directions *From Sacramento: Go east on Highway 50. Exit east on Highway 16 about 21 miles to the golf course.*

RANCHO MURIETA COUNTRY CLUB—NORTH

Quality Rating 93

Value Rating C

RANCHO MURIETA COUNTRY CLUB—NORTH

Address	14813 Jackson Road
City, Zip	Rancho Murieta, 95683
Telephone	(916) 985–7200
Ownership	Resort
Weekday Fee	$55
Weekend Fee	$55
Twilight Fee	—

Men's Par	72
Men's Yardage	6307
Men's Rating	71.7
Women's Par	72
Women's Yardage	5339
Women's Rating	72.8
Championship Yardage	6875
Championship Rating	73.7

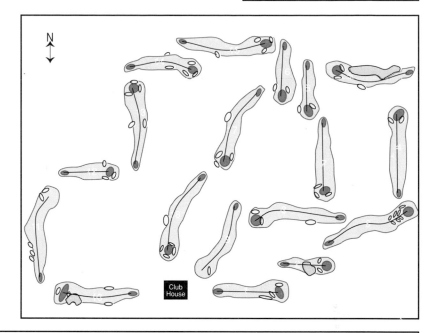

OVERALL APPEAL	Outstanding	15	of possible	15
DESIGN & VARIETY	Outstanding	15	of possible	15
SCENERY	Very Good	12	of possible	15
OVERALL DIFFICULTY	Outstanding	10	of possible	10
GREENS DIFFICULTY	Outstanding	10	of possible	10
OVERALL CONDITION	Very Good	8	of possible	10
GREENS CONDITION	Very Good	8	of possible	10
HAZARDS	Outstanding	10	of possible	10
COSMETICS	Outstanding	5	of possible	5
TOTAL	**Outstanding**	**93**	**of possible**	**100**

Description This course has rolling hills with narrow to medium-wide fairways bordered by mature oak trees. It is located in the lower foothills. The front side meanders through the hills with beautiful oak trees. The back side weaves through an attractive residential area. Trees, many contoured bunkers, and lakes provide the hazards. It has a lot of "picture-perfect" golf holes. A country club atmosphere prevails. 2nd BEST COSMETICS 3rd BEST PRACTICE FACILITIES 4th BEST CLUBHOUSE 4th MOST DIFFICULT GREENS 7th BEST DESIGN 7th MOST DIFFICULT COURSE 7th BEST FINISHING HOLE 9th BEST GREENS CONDITION

QUALITY RANKING 8th   VALUE RANKING 78th

Clubhouse Facilities EXCELLENT Pro shop, snack bar, full bar, fine dining, banquet

Practice Facilities EXCELLENT Driving range, putting green, chipping green, bunkers

Who Should Play Everyone, at least once; then, those looking for a challenge

Walkability Carts are mandatory

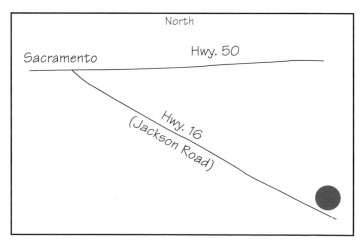

Directions *From Sacramento: Go east on Highway 50. Exit east on Highway 16 about 21 miles to the golf course.*

ALTA SIERRA GOLF & COUNTRY CLUB

Poor	Below Average	Average	Good	Very Good	Outstanding
☐	☐	■	☐	☐	☐

Quality Rating	**45**
Value Rating	**D**

ALTA SIERRA GOLF & COUNTRY CLUB

Address	144 Tammy Way
City, Zip	Grass Valley, 95949
Telephone	(916) 273–2010
Ownership	Independent
Weekday Fee	$17
Weekend Fee	$20
Twilight Fee	—

Men's Par	72
Men's Yardage	6263
Men's Rating	70.1
Women's Par	72
Women's Yardage	5919
Women's Rating	73.9
Championship Yardage	6469
Championship Rating	71.3

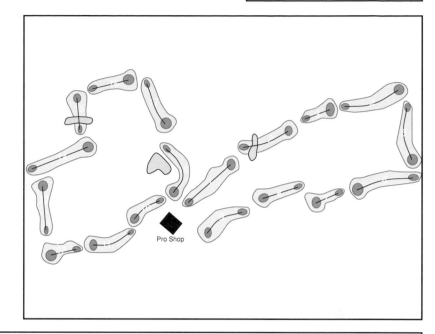

OVERALL APPEAL	Poor	0	of possible	15
DESIGN & VARIETY	Good	9	of possible	15
SCENERY	Very Good	12	of possible	15
OVERALL DIFFICULTY	Good	6	of possible	10
GREENS DIFFICULTY	Average	4	of possible	10
OVERALL CONDITION	Poor	0	of possible	10
GREENS CONDITION	Good	6	of possible	10
HAZARDS	Very Good	8	of possible	10
COSMETICS	Poor	0	of possible	5
TOTAL	**Average**	**45**	**of possible**	**100**

Description This course is hilly with narrow to medium-wide fairways bordered by mature pine and oak trees. It is located near 2,200 feet in elevation and weaves through a residential area. Trees, bunkers, and some water provide the hazards. It is in a beautiful location and offers a really fun design. However, negligent maintenance prevails. With proper upkeep, it could be a very good course to play.

QUALITY RANKING 76th   VALUE RANKING 87th
Clubhouse Facilities   FAIR Pro shop, snack bar, full bar, coffee shop
Practice Facilities   POOR Driving range, putting green
Who Should Play Those looking for convenience

Walkability Difficult

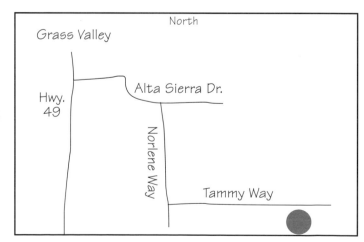

Directions *Go south on Highway 49 about 7 miles. Go east on Alta Sierra Drive about 2 miles. Go south on Norlene Way about 1 mile. Go east on Tammy Way to the golf course.*

AHOE DONNER GOLF & COUNTRY CLUB

Poor	Below Average	Average	Good	Very Good	Outstanding
☐	☐	☐	☐	■	☐

Quality Rating 87

Value Rating C

TAHOE DONNER GOLF & COUNTRY CLUB

Address	Northwoods Boulevard
City, Zip	Truckee, 95734
Telephone	(916) 587–9440
Ownership	Independent
Weekday Fee	$34
Weekend Fee	$41
Twilight Fee	$17

Men's Par	72
Men's Yardage	6635
Men's Rating	71.5
Women's Par	74
Women's Yardage	6025
Women's Rating	73.5
Championship Yardage	6961
Championship Rating	73.3

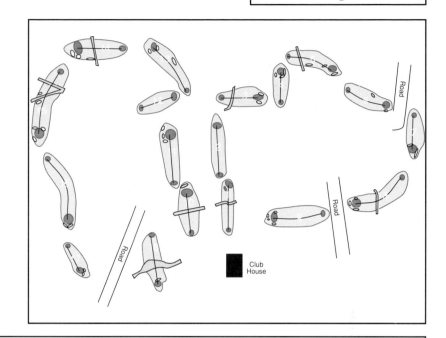

OVERALL APPEAL	Outstanding	15	of possible	15
DESIGN & VARIETY	Outstanding	15	of possible	15
SCENERY	Outstanding	15	of possible	15
OVERALL DIFFICULTY	Outstanding	10	of possible	10
GREENS DIFFICULTY	Very Good	8	of possible	10
OVERALL CONDITION	Very Good	8	of possible	10
GREENS CONDITION	Average	4	of possible	10
HAZARDS	Very Good	8	of possible	10
COSMETICS	Very Good	4	of possible	5
TOTAL	**Very Good**	**87**	**of possible**	**100**

Description   This course has rolling hills with narrow to medium-wide fairways. It weaves through a beautiful pine forest with no side-by-side fairways. Some upscale homes border the fairways. Dense trees, bunkers, and some water provide the hazards. It is a beautiful and exciting course to play. Management takes pride in the facilities. 2nd BEST "FUN COURSE" 5th BEST SCENERY 8th BEST FINISHING HOLE 10th MOST DIFFICULT COURSE

QUALITY RANKING   13th   VALUE RANKING   64th
Clubhouse Facilities   FAIR   Pro shop, snack bar, coffee shop, full bar
Practice Facilities   POOR   Driving range, putting green
Who Should Play   Everyone

Walkability   Moderate

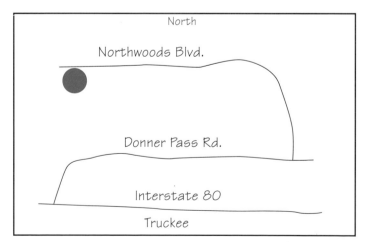

Directions   *From I80: Exit north on the Truckee exit to Donner Pass Road. Go north on Northwoods Boulevard about 2 miles to the golf course.*

167

Quality Rating 64

Value Rating D

NORTHSTAR AT TAHOE
RESORT GOLF COURSE

Address	Basque Drive
City, Zip	Truckee, 95734
Telephone	(916) 587–0290
Ownership	Resort
Weekday Fee	$30
Weekend Fee	$30
Twilight Fee	$18

Men's Par	72
Men's Yardage	6015
Men's Rating	67.4
Women's Par	72
Women's Yardage	5491
Women's Rating	70.3
Championship Yardage	6897
Championship Rating	72

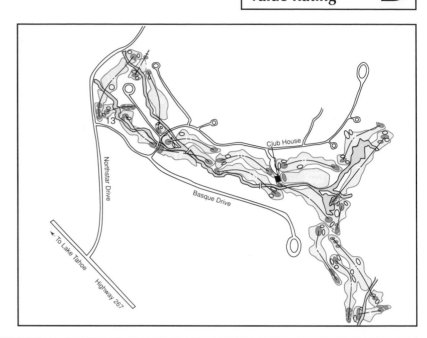

OVERALL APPEAL	Average	6	of possible	15
DESIGN & VARIETY	Average	6	of possible	15
SCENERY	Outstanding	15	of possible	15
OVERALL DIFFICULTY	Outstanding	10	of possible	10
GREENS DIFFICULTY	Very Good	8	of possible	10
OVERALL CONDITION	Average	4	of possible	10
GREENS CONDITION	Below Average	2	of possible	10
HAZARDS	Outstanding	10	of possible	10
COSMETICS	Good	3	of possible	5
TOTAL	**Good**	**64**	**of possible**	**100**

Description The front side is completely different from the back side. The front side has medium-wide fairways with almost no trees. It is located in an open meadow with panoramic views of the surrounding mountains. Bunkers and lakes provide the hazards. The back side is located in the forest with some residential housing. Very narrow fairways, hills, bunkers, ravines, and water provide the hazards. There are beautiful pine and aspen trees on this side. 6th BEST SCORECARD

QUALITY RANKING 41st VALUE RANKING 83rd
Clubhouse Facilities GOOD Pro shop, coffee shop, full bar
Practice Facilities FAIR Matted driving range, 2 putting greens
Who Should Play Front side—everyone; back side—low handicappers and those looking for scenery
Walkability Moderate

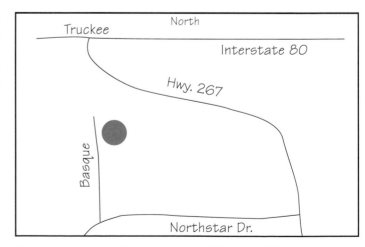

Directions *From I80: Exit south on Highway 267 about 6 miles. Go west on Northstar Drive. Go north on Basque to the golf course.*

| Poor | Below Average | Average | Good | Very Good | Outstanding |

Quality Rating 80

Value Rating A

FALL RIVER VALLEY GOLF & COUNTRY CLUB

Address	Highway 299E
City, Zip	Fall River Mills, 96028
Telephone	(916) 336–5555
Ownership	Independent
Weekday Fee	$10
Weekend Fee	$14
Twilight Fee	—

Men's Par	72
Men's Yardage	6826
Men's Rating	71.3
Women's Par	72
Women's Yardage	6257
Women's Rating	—
Championship Yardage	7333
Championship Rating	75.2

OVERALL APPEAL	Outstanding	15	of possible	15
DESIGN & VARIETY	Outstanding	15	of possible	15
SCENERY	Outstanding	15	of possible	15
OVERALL DIFFICULTY	Outstanding	10	of possible	10
GREENS DIFFICULTY	Good	6	of possible	10
OVERALL CONDITION	Average	4	of possible	10
GREENS CONDITION	Average	4	of possible	10
HAZARDS	Outstanding	10	of possible	10
COSMETICS	Below Average	1	of possible	5
TOTAL	**Very Good**	**80**	**of possible**	**100**

Description   This golf course has rolling hills with wide fairways bordered by mature pine trees. It is located on the rugged plateau near Mt. Lassen. Some residential housing and open land surrounds the course. Trees, bunkers, strategically placed lakes, and sagebrush provide the hazards. The holes weave through the forest and open land. The course is exceptionally well designed with many interesting holes—a "diamond-in-the-rough." 4th MOST DIFFICULT COURSE 7th BEST "FUN COURSE" 9th BEST HAZARDS 10th BEST FINISHING HOLE

QUALITY RANKING   19th   VALUE RANKING   2nd
Clubhouse Facilities   FAIR   Pro shop, coffee shop, full bar
Practice Facilities   FAIR   Driving range, putting green

Who Should Play   Everyone

Walkability   Moderate

North

Hwy. 299 E

Fall River Mills

Directions   *Go west on Highway 299 about 1 mile to the golf course.*

GRAEAGLE MEADOWS GOLF COURSE

□		□		□		■		□		□
Poor	Below Average	Average	Good	Very Good	Outstanding

GRAEAGLE MEADOWS GOLF COURSE

Address	P.O. Box 124
City, Zip	Graeagle, 96103
Telephone	(916) 836–2323
Ownership	Independent
Weekday Fee	$17
Weekend Fee	$20
Twilight Fee	$10

Men's Par	72
Men's Yardage	6668
Men's Rating	70.7
Women's Par	72
Women's Yardage	5652
Women's Rating	69.9
Championship Yardage	—
Championship Rating	—

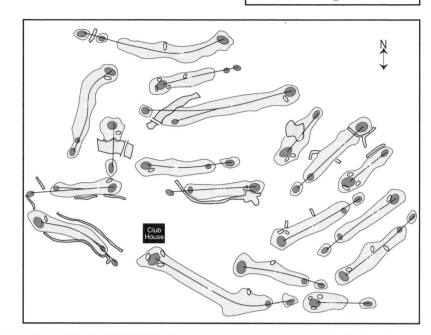

OVERALL APPEAL	Very Good	12	of possible	15
DESIGN & VARIETY	Very Good	12	of possible	15
SCENERY	Outstanding	15	of possible	15
OVERALL DIFFICULTY	Very Good	8	of possible	10
GREENS DIFFICULTY	Good	6	of possible	10
OVERALL CONDITION	Average	4	of possible	10
GREENS CONDITION	Average	4	of possible	10
HAZARDS	Good	6	of possible	10
COSMETICS	Very Good	4	of possible	5
TOTAL	**Good**	**71**	**of possible**	**100**

Description   This course is flat with a few hills. Fairways are narrow to wide and bordered by mature pine trees. The course is located in a mountain meadow with beautiful, panoramic views. Some residential homes surround one side and open land surrounds the other. Trees, bunkers, marsh, lakes, and the Feather River provide the hazards. Many interesting holes, beautiful scenery, and very good challenge make for an enjoyable round of golf. With improved maintenance, it could be a very good golf course.

QUALITY RANKING   32nd   VALUE RANKING   41st
Clubhouse Facilities   FAIR   Pro shop, snack bar, full bar
Practice Facilities   FAIR   Driving range, putting green

Who Should Play   Everyone

Walkability   Moderate

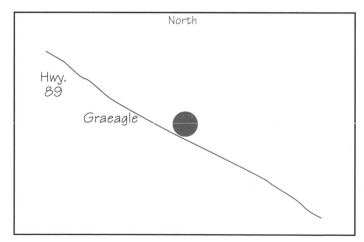

Directions   *In Graeagle: Go south on Highway 89 about ½ mile to the golf course.*

Poor	Below Average	Average	Good	Very Good	Outstanding
☐	☐	☐	■	☐	☐

Quality Rating	**60**
Value Rating	**D**

PLUMAS PINES COUNTRY CLUB

Address	402 Poplar Valley Road
City, Zip	Blairsden, 96103
Telephone	(916) 836–1420
Ownership	Independent
Weekday Fee	$26
Weekend Fee	$26
Twilight Fee	$16

Men's Par	72
Men's Yardage	5843
Men's Rating	68.0
Women's Par	70
Women's Yardage	4995
Women's Rating	67.3
Championship Yardage	6365
Championship Rating	70.6

OVERALL APPEAL	Average	6	of possible	15
DESIGN & VARIETY	Below Average	3	of possible	15
SCENERY	Outstanding	15	of possible	15
OVERALL DIFFICULTY	Good	6	of possible	10
GREENS DIFFICULTY	Average	4	of possible	10
OVERALL CONDITION	Very Good	8	of possible	10
GREENS CONDITION	Good	6	of possible	10
HAZARDS	Very Good	8	of possible	10
COSMETICS	Very Good	4	of possible	5
TOTAL	**Good**	**60**	**of possible**	**100**

Description   This course is hilly with narrow fairways bordered by mature pine trees. It is located at the 4,500 mark in elevation and is surrounded by residential housing and open land. Trees, bunkers, lakes, and the Feather River provide the hazards. The front side weaves through the forest and the back side is in a meadow. Most of the holes play quite short. Management takes pride in the facilities. 7th BEST SCENERY 9th BEST OVERALL CONDITION 10th BEST COSMETICS 10th BEST CLUBHOUSE

QUALITY RANKING   47th   VALUE RANKING   81st

Clubhouse Facilities   EXCELLENT   Pro shop, snack bar, full bar, coffee shop, fine dining

Practice Facilities   FAIR   Driving range, putting green

Who Should Play   High handicappers and those looking for scenery

Walkability   Difficult

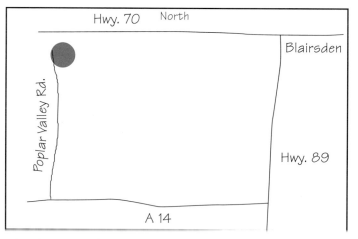

Directions   *In Blairsden: Go south on Highway 89 about 1 mile. Go west on County Road A14 about 2 miles. Go north on Poplar Valley Road to golf course.*

173

LAKE SHASTINA GOLF RESORT

Poor	Below Average	Average	Good	Very Good	Outstanding
☐	☐	☐	☐	■	☐

LAKE SHASTINA GOLF RESORT

Address	5925 Country Club Drive
City, Zip	Weed, 96094
Telephone	(916) 938–3201
Ownership	Resort
Weekday Fee	$28
Weekend Fee	$28
Twilight Fee	$14

Men's Par	72
Men's Yardage	6291
Men's Rating	69.5
Women's Par	72
Women's Yardage	5530
Women's Rating	70.2
Championship Yardage	6969
Championship Rating	72.6

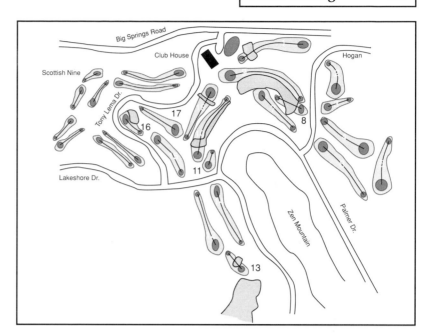

OVERALL APPEAL	Outstanding	15	of possible	15
DESIGN & VARIETY	Outstanding	15	of possible	15
SCENERY	Outstanding	15	of possible	15
OVERALL DIFFICULTY	Outstanding	10	of possible	10
GREENS DIFFICULTY	Very Good	8	of possible	10
OVERALL CONDITION	Good	6	of possible	10
GREENS CONDITION	Very Good	8	of possible	10
HAZARDS	Outstanding	10	of possible	10
COSMETICS	Average	2	of possible	5
TOTAL	**Very Good**	. **89**	**of possible**	**100**

Description   This course is flat with a few small hills. It has narrow to wide fairways bordered by mature pine trees. It is located near Mt. Shasta with residential housing surrounding the course. The front side weaves through the forest and the back side is out in the open with lots of sagebrush between the holes. Trees, water, and strategically placed bunkers provide the hazards. It is a very challenging and fun course to play. It's exceptionally well designed for all levels of players.

QUALITY RANKING   11th   VALUE RANKING   48th
Clubhouse Facilities   GOOD   Pro shop, snack bar, full bar, fine dining
Practice Facilities   FAIR   Driving range, 2 putting greens
Who Should Play   Everyone

Walkability   Moderate

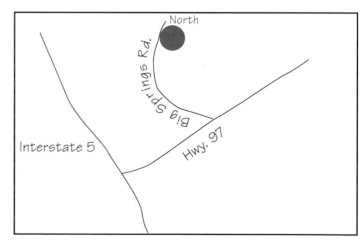

Directions   *From I5: Exit north on Highway 97 about 4 miles. Go west on Big Springs Road for about 3 miles to the golf course.*

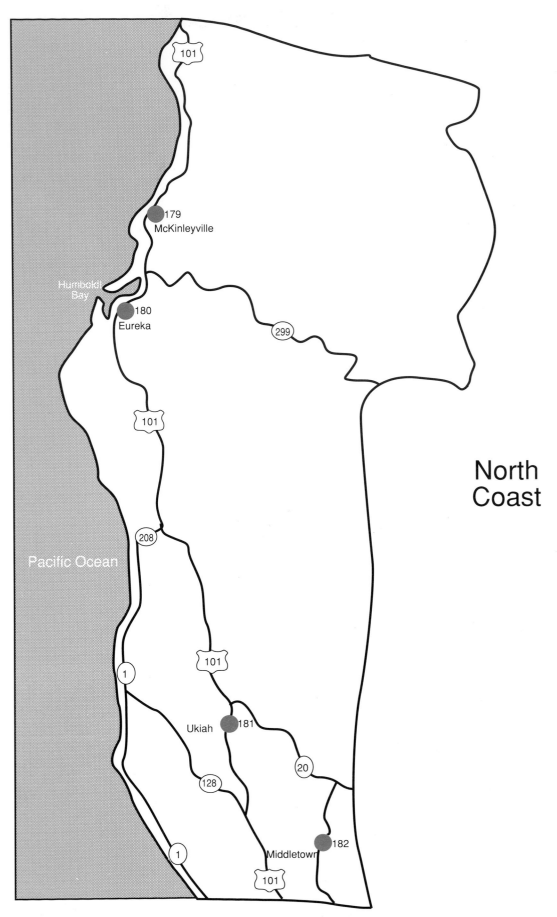

North
Coast

Numbered dots indicate the page number where the golf course is described.

NORTH COAST

The North Coast zone is a vast area of land from the Pacific Ocean in the west to the Central Valley in the east and from the Oregon/California border in the north to just south of Clear Lake at Middletown. Most of this terrain is very rugged. It ranges from the beautiful California coastline to many deep and remote canyons. Unfortunately, golf is not a high-priority activity, as only four 18-hole public courses are offered. With one exception, these courses are located in the largest towns.

Weather conditions are moderate, making golf possible on a year-round basis. Summertime is the best time of the year to play. Winter will have many days of rain. Courses near the ocean can get very windy and cold at times. Be sure to take a sweater and windbreaker when you play golf in this zone.

All the courses are inexpensive and informal golf attire is acceptable. Unfortunately, these courses need improvement in their maintenance. Tee times are not really needed except during peak hours on the weekends and mornings.

BEAU PRE GOLF CLUB

| Poor | Below Average | Average | Good | Very Good | Outstanding |

| | | | | | | | Quality Rating | **52** |
| Poor | Below Average | Average | Good | Very Good | Outstanding | | Value Rating | **C** |

BEAU PRE GOLF CLUB

Address   1777 Norton Road
City, Zip   McKinleyville, 95521
Telephone   (707) 839–2342
Ownership   Independent
Weekday Fee $9
Weekend Fee $12
Twilight Fee $6

Men's Par   71
Men's Yardage   5346
Men's Rating   66.2
Women's Par   71
Women's Yardage   4882
Women's Rating   66.4
Championship
    Yardage   5651
Championship
    Rating   66.6

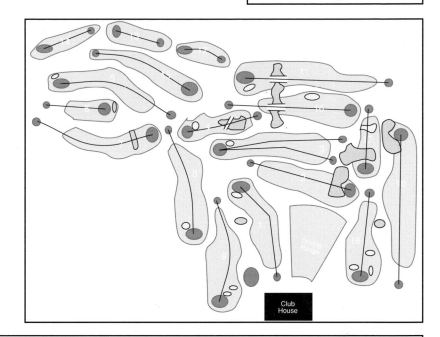

OVERALL APPEAL	Good	9	of possible	15
DESIGN & VARIETY	Good	9	of possible	15
SCENERY	Outstanding	15	of possible	15
OVERALL DIFFICULTY	Average	4	of possible	10
GREENS DIFFICULTY	Below Average	2	of possible	10
OVERALL CONDITION	Below Average	2	of possible	10
GREENS CONDITION	Below Average	2	of possible	10
HAZARDS	Very Good	8	of possible	10
COSMETICS	Below Average	1	of possible	5
TOTAL	**Average**	**52**	**of possible**	**100**

Description   This course is flat, with a few hills. Fairways are narrow to medium-wide bordered by middle-aged to mature pine trees. Open land and some residential housing surround the course. Trees, bunkers, and strategically placed water provide the hazards. Some of the holes are flat and rather average. Other holes are into the hills and wind through the beautiful forest with distant views of the ocean. It could be a good course with improved maintenance.

QUALITY RANKING   61st   VALUE RANKING   36th
Clubhouse Facilities   FAIR   Pro shop, snack bar

Practice Facilities   FAIR   Matted driving range, putting green, chipping green
Who Should Play   Everyone

Walkability   Difficult

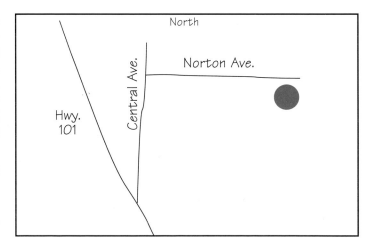

Directions   *From Highway 101: Exit north on Central Avenue about ½ mile. Go east on Norton Road to golf course.*

Poor	Below Average	Average	Good	Very Good	Outstanding
☐	■	☐	☐	☐	☐

Quality Rating	33
Value Rating	C

EUREKA MUNICIPAL GOLF COURSE

Address   4750 Fairway Drive
City, Zip   Eureka, 95501
Telephone   (707) 443–4808
Ownership   Municipal
Weekday Fee $6.50
Weekend Fee $8
Twilight Fee $4

Men's Par   70
Men's Yardage   5589
Men's Rating   66.5
Women's Par   70
Women's Yardage   5320
Women's Rating   69.4
Championship
   Yardage   5868
Championship
   Rating   —

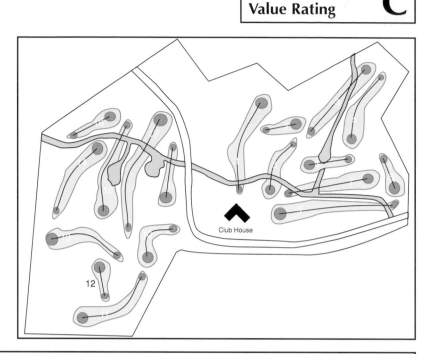

OVERALL APPEAL	Below Average	3	of possible	15
DESIGN & VARIETY	Average	6	of possible	15
SCENERY	Very Good	12	of possible	15
OVERALL DIFFICULTY	Average	4	of possible	10
GREENS DIFFICULTY	Below Average	2	of possible	10
OVERALL CONDITION	Poor	0	of possible	10
GREENS CONDITION	Poor	0	of possible	10
HAZARDS	Good	6	of possible	10
COSMETICS	Poor	0	of possible	5
TOTAL	**Below Average**	**33**	**of possible**	**100**

Description This course has rolling hills with narrow to wide fairways bordered by pine and a variety of middle-aged to mature trees. It is surrounded by open land and forest. Trees, bunkers, and strategically placed streams and water provide the hazards. It has a beautiful location with some interesting holes. However, negligent maintenance brings the appeal of this course down significantly.

QUALITY RANKING 94th   VALUE RANKING   77th
Clubhouse Facilities   FAIR   Pro shop, snack bar

Practice Facilities   POOR   Driving range, putting green
Who Should Play   Those looking for convenience

Walkability   Moderate

180

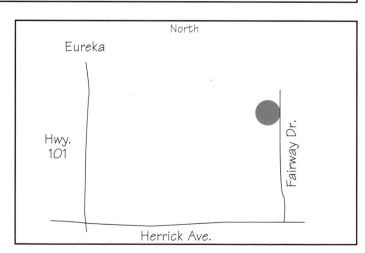

Directions   *Go south on Highway 101. Exit east on Herrick. Go north on Fairway Drive to the golf course.*

Poor	Below Average	Average	Good	Very Good	Outstanding
☐	☐	■	☐	☐	☐

UKIAH MUNICIPAL GOLF COURSE

Address	Park Boulevard
City, Zip	Ukiah, 95482
Telephone	(702) 462–8857
Ownership	Municipal
Weekday Fee	$7
Weekend Fee	$9
Twilight Fee	—

Men's Par	70
Men's Yardage	5612
Men's Rating	66.5
Women's Par	70
Women's Yardage	5334
Women's Rating	69.4
Championship Yardage	5833
Championship Rating	67.6

OVERALL APPEAL	Average	6	of possible	15
DESIGN & VARIETY	Below Average	3	of possible	15
SCENERY	Outstanding	15	of possible	15
OVERALL DIFFICULTY	Average	4	of possible	10
GREENS DIFFICULTY	Below Average	2	of possible	10
OVERALL CONDITION	Below Average	2	of possible	10
GREENS CONDITION	Average	4	of possible	10
HAZARDS	Average	4	of possible	10
COSMETICS	Average	2	of possible	5
TOTAL	**Average**	**42**	**of possible**	**100**

Description This course is hilly with narrow to wide fairways bordered by young to mature oak and pine trees. It is surrounded by residential housing and hills. Trees, bunkers, and some water provide the hazards. It's a short course with a few interesting holes. Some holes aren't very well designed. There are some elevated tee boxes with excellent views of the valley below.

QUALITY RANKING 84th   VALUE RANKING 33rd
Clubhouse Facilities   POOR   Snack bar, pro shop

Practice Facilities   POOR   Driving range, putting green
Who Should Play   Everyone

Walkability   Difficult

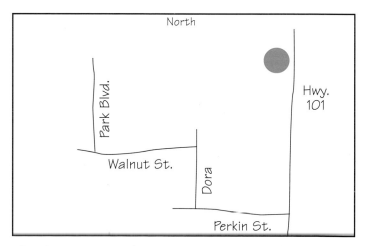

Directions   *From Highway 101: Exit west on Perkin Street. Go north on Dora. Go west on Walnut Street. Go north on Park Boulevard to the golf course.*

| Poor | Below Average | Average | Good | Very Good | Outstanding |

Quality Rating **33**

Value Rating **D**

HIDDEN VALLEY GOLF & COUNTRY CLUB

Address	P.O. Box 628
City, Zip	Middletown, 95461
Telephone	(707) 987–3035
Ownership	Independent
Weekday Fee	$10
Weekend Fee	$17
Twilight Fee	—

Men's Par	72
Men's Yardage	6237
Men's Rating	69.5
Women's Par	75
Women's Yardage	5666
Women's Rating	72.0
Championship Yardage	6590
Championship Rating	71.1

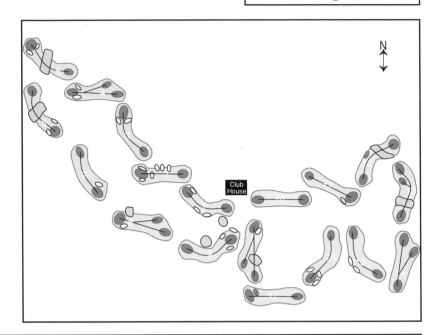

OVERALL APPEAL	Poor	0	of possible	15
DESIGN & VARIETY	Poor	0	of possible	15
SCENERY	Good	9	of possible	15
OVERALL DIFFICULTY	Good	6	of possible	10
GREENS DIFFICULTY	Good	6	of possible	10
OVERALL CONDITION	Below Average	2	of possible	10
GREENS CONDITION	Good	6	of possible	10
HAZARDS	Average	4	of possible	10
COSMETICS	Poor	0	of possible	5
TOTAL	**Below Average**	**33**	**of possible**	**100**

Description This course is flat with a few very steep hills. Fairways are medium to wide bordered by mature oak trees. Residential housing surrounds the course. Trees, bunkers, and some water provide the hazards. Most of the holes are flat and boring to play. Four golf holes wind through the hills and are a bit more interesting. There is not much imagination to this course except for one hole where the tee box is greatly elevated above the fairway.

QUALITY RANKING 96th VALUE RANKING 98th
Clubhouse Facilities FAIR Snack bar, pro shop, coffee shop, full bar
Practice Facilities FAIR Driving range, putting green

Who Should Play Those looking for convenience

Walkability Front side is easy, back side is difficult

182

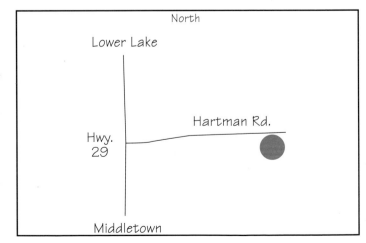

Directions *Go north on Highway 29 about 5 miles. Go east on Hartman Road to the golf course.*

TRIVIA QUESTIONS

The trivia questions in this chapter are based on the golf courses rated in this guidebook. Test yourself and your friends on your knowledge of Northern California's 18-hole, public, regulation golf courses. Please turn to "Trivia Answers" to check your responses.

1. What golf course has the longest par 5 hole?
2. What two golf courses begin with par 3's?
3. What six golf complexes have two 18-hole courses?
4. What golf course has Dr. Alister McKenzie's, the famous architect, favorite hole?
5. What golf course is "home" to the Northern California Golf Association?
6. What golf course has the name of a fruit in its name?
7. What golf course is closest to Yosemite National Park?
8. What golf course's name means "Beautiful Prairie"?
9. Currently, what two golf courses host a PGA Tour tournament each year?
10. What golf course has the longest par 4 hole?
11. What golf course has an unobstructed view of the Golden Gate Bridge?
12. What golf course has no sand traps and only one grass bunker?
13. What golf course is located on the banks of the Tuolumne River?
14. What golf course has a precious stone in its name?
15. What golf course in wintertime uses its fairways as a snowmobile area?
16. What golf course is surrounded on three sides by a lake?
17. What golf course has the longest par 3 hole?
18. What golf course constructed a man-made levee to protect itself from the ocean?
19. What golf course uses an old house as a clubhouse?
20. What two golf courses have an island green?
21. What golf course calls itself "The Magnificent Monster"?
22. What golf course has a wooden walkway through a marsh?
23. What ski resort offers a golf resort in the summertime?
24. What golf course has a precious metal in its name?
25. What golf course did Ronald Reagan build the Governor's Mansion next to?
26. What golf course calls itself "The Sunshine Course"?

27. What golf course has the shortest par 5 hole?
28. What golf course has a bird in its name?
29. What eight golf courses end with a par 3 hole?
30. At what golf course can sailboarders interfere with golfers?
31. What golf course has full, liquor bars *on* the golf course?
32. What golf course has a funicular transporting golfers to the next tee box?
33. What golf course, in its original position, is the oldest course west of the Mississippi?
34. What three golf courses name their golf holes?
35. What golf course has the shortest par 4 hole?
36. What golf course has views of some of the highest mountains in the United States?
37. What golf course is the Senior PGA Tour's "Senior Gold Rush" tournament played on?
38. What golf course has a par 6 hole?
39. What golf course's coffee shop uses antique golf clubs as wall decorations?
40. What golf course surrounds a famous lighthouse?
41. What golf course has three flags on one green?
42. What golf course is located across the highway from a weapons storage area?
43. What golf course has the shortest par 3 hole?
44. What golf course has *no* snack bar, coffee shop, or restaurant?
45. What golf course has palm trees surrounding all 18 greens?
46. What two golf courses have holes where the ocean or bluffs come directly into play?
47. What golf course is located on an island?
48. What golf course has the longest finishing hole?
49. How many of Northern California's public, 18-hole, regulation golf courses have you played?

TOP TEN BEST COURSES

1. **SPYGLASS HILL GOLF COURSE (100)**

   1st Best Design
   1st Most Difficult Course
   1st Best Overall Condition
   1st Best Greens Condition
   2nd Best Scenery
   2nd Most Difficult Greens
   2nd Best Hazards
   2nd Best Scorecard
   4th Best Cosmetics

2. **POPPY HILLS GOLF COURSE (99)**

   2nd Best Overall Condition
   2nd Best Greens Condition
   3rd Best Scenery
   3rd Best Hazards
   3rd Most Difficult Course
   3rd Most Difficult Greens
   4th Best Design
   5th Best Clubhouse
   6th Best Practice Facilities
   9th Best Scorecard

3. **PEBBLE BEACH GOLF LINKS (98)**

   1st Best Scenery
   1st Best Finishing Hole
   1st Best Clubhouse
   3rd Best Cosmetics
   3rd Best Scorecard
   5th Most Difficult Course

   5th Most Difficult Greens
   5th Best Greens Condition
   6th Best Design
   7th Best Overall Condition
   7th Best Hazards

4. **CANYON LAKES COUNTRY CLUB (98)**

   3rd Best Overall Condition
   4rd Best Overall Condition
   4th Best "Fun Course"
   6th Best Cosmetics
   9th Best Design

5. **FOUNTAINGROVE COUNTRY CLUB (96)**

   1st Best Cosmetics
   3rd Best Clubhouse
   7th Most Difficult Greens
   8th Best Hazards
   8th Best Design
   9th Most Difficult Course
   10th Best Practice Facilities

6. **PASATIEMPO GOLF CLUB (94)**

   4th Best Practice Facilities
   5th Best Design
   5th Best Hazards
   5th Best Cosmetics
   6th Best "Fun Course"
   8th Most Difficult Greens
   8th Best Overall Condition

7. CHARDONNAY CLUB (94)

2nd Best Design
3rd Best "Fun Course"
4th Best Hazards
5th Best Finishing Hole
6th Most Difficult Greens
8th Most Difficult Course
10th Best Greens Condition

8. RANCHO MURIETA C.C.—NORTH (93)

2nd Best Cosmetics
3rd Best Practice Facilities
4th Best Clubhouse
4th Most Difficult Greens
7th Best Design
7th Most Difficult Course
7th Best Finishing Hole
9th Best Greens Condition

9. THE LINKS AT SPANISH BAY (92)

1st Best Hazards
1st Most Difficult Greens
2nd Most Difficult Course
2nd Best Clubhouse
3rd Best Design
3rd Best Finishing Hole
4th Best Scenery
4th Best Scorecard
8th Best Cosmetics

10. HALF MOON BAY GOLF LINKS (90)

2nd Best Finishing Hole
5th Best Scorecard
6th Most Difficult Course
8th Best "Fun Course"
10th Best Design
10th Best Hazards

TOP TEN LISTS BY CATEGORY

FUN COURSE*

1. Aptos Seascape Golf Course

2. Tahoe Donner Golf & C.C.
3. Chardonnay Club
4. Canyon Lakes Country Club
5. Harding Park Golf Course
6. Pasatiempo Golf Club
7. Fall River Valley Golf & C.C.
8. Half Moon Bay Golf Links
9. Pajaro Valley Golf Club
10. Rancho Murieta C.C.—South

BEST SCENERY

1. Pebble Beach Golf Links

2. Spyglass Hill Golf Course
3. Poppy Hills Golf Course
4. The Links at Spanish Bay
5. Tahoe Donner Golf & C.C.
6. Lincoln Park Golf Course
7. Plumas Pines Country Club
8. Harding Park Golf Course
9. Lake Chabot Golf Course
10. Bodega Harbour Golf Links

BEST DESIGN

1. Spyglass Hill Golf Course

2. Chardonnay Club
3. The Links at Spanish Bay
4. Poppy Hills Golf Course

5. Pasatiempo Golf Club
6. Pebble Beach Golf Links
7. Rancho Murieta C.C.—North
8. Fountaingrove Country Club
9. Canyon Lakes Country Club
10. Half Moon Bay Golf Links

MOST DIFFICULT

1. Spyglass Hill Golf Course

2. The Links at Spanish Bay
3. Poppy Hills Golf Course
4. Fall River Valley Golf & C.C.
5. Pebble Beach Golf Links
6. Half Moon Bay Golf Links
7. Rancho Murieta C.C.—North
8. Chardonnay Club
9. Fountaingrove Country Club
10. Tahoe Donner Golf & C.C.

MOST DIFFICULT GREENS

1. The Links at Spanish Bay

2. Spyglass Hill Golf Course
3. Poppy Hills Golf Course
4. Rancho Murieta C.C.—North
5. Pebble Beach Golf Links
6. Chardonnay Club
7. Fountaingrove Country Club
8. Pasatiempo Golf Club
9. Bodega Harbour Golf Links
10. Shoreline Golf Course

*A fun course is a golf course that's enjoyable to play everyday.

BEST GREENS CONDITION

1. Spyglass Hill Golf Course

2. Poppy Hills Golf Course
3. Oakmont Golf Course—West
4. Canyon Lakes Country Club
5. Pebble Beach Golf Links
6. Palo Alto Municipal Golf Course
7. Rancho Cañada Golf Club—East
8. Rancho Cañada Golf Club—West
9. Rancho Murieta C.C.—North
10. Chardonnay Club

BEST OVERALL CONDITION

1. Spyglass Hill Golf Course

2. Poppy Hills Golf Course
3. Canyon Lakes Country Club
4. Ridgemark C.C.—Diablo
5. Palo Alto Municipal G.C.
6. Shoreline Golf Course
7. Pebble Beach Golf Links
8. Pasatiempo Golf Club
9. Plumas Pines Country Club
10. Ridgemark C.C.—Gabilan

BEST HAZARDS

1. The Links at Spanish Bay

2. Spyglass Hill Golf Course
3. Poppy Hills Golf Course
4. Chardonnay Club
5. Pasatiempo Golf Club
6. Bodega Harbour Golf Links
7. Pebble Beach Golf Links
8. Fountaingrove Country Club
9. Fall River Valley Golf & C.C.
10. Half Moon Bay Golf Links

BEST COSMETICS

1. Fountaingrove Country Club

2. Rancho Murieta C.C.—North
3. Pebble Beach Golf Links
4. Spyglass Hill Golf Course
5. Pasatiempo Golf Club
6. Canyon Lakes Country Club
7. Rancho Cañada Golf Club—East
8. The Links at Spanish Bay
9. Rancho Cañada Golf Club—West
10. Plumas Pines Country Club

188

BEST PRACTICE FACILITIES

1. Santa Clara Golf & Tennis Club

2. Santa Teresa Golf Club
3. Rancho Murieta Country Club
4. Pasatiempo Golf Club
5. Rancho Cañada Golf Club
6. Poppy Hills Golf Course
7. Oakmont Golf Course—West
8. Palo Alto Municipal G.C.
9. Haggin Oaks Golf Course
10. Fountaingrove Country Club

BEST CLUBHOUSE

1. Pebble Beach Golf Links

2. The Links at Spanish Bay
3. Fountaingrove Country Club
4. Rancho Murieta Country Club—North
5. Poppy Hills Golf Course
6. Aptos Seascape Golf Course
7. Ridgemark Country Club
8. Oakmont Golf Course
9. Santa Clara Golf & Tennis Club
10. Plumas Pines Country Club

BEST SCORECARD

1. Del Monte Golf Course

2. Spyglass Hill Golf Course
3. Pebble Beach Golf Links
4. The Links at Spanish Bay
5. Half Moon Bay Golf Links
6. Northstar at Tahoe Resort G.C.
7. Fresno West Golf & C.C.
8. Palo Alto Municipal G.C.
9. Poppy Hills Golf Course
10. Shoreline Golf Course

BEST FINISHING HOLE

1. Pebble Beach Golf Links

2. Half Moon Bay Golf Links
3. The Links at Spanish Bay
4. Bodega Harbour Golf Links
5. Chardonnay Club
6. Fig Garden Golf Club
7. Rancho Murieta C.C.—North
8. Tahoe Dinner Golf & C.C.
9. Mountain Shadows Golf Course—North
10. Fall River Valley Golf & C.C.

NORTHERN CALIFORNIA'S QUALITY RANKINGS

OUTSTANDING

RANK	QUALITY	GOLF COURSE
1.	100	Spyglass Hill Golf Course
2.	99	Poppy Hills Golf Course
3.	98	Pebble Beach Golf Links
4.	98	Canyon Lakes Country Club
5.	96	Fountaingrove Country Club
6.	94	Pasatiempo Golf Club
7.	94	Chardonnay Club
8.	93	Rancho Murieta Country Club—North
9.	92	The Links at Spanish Bay

VERY GOOD

RANK	QUALITY	GOLF COURSE
10.	90	Half Moon Bay Golf Links
11.	89	Lake Shastina Golf Resort
12.	88	Oakmont Golf Course—West
13.	87	Tahoe Donner Golf & Country Club
14.	85	Bodega Harbour Golf Links
15.	83	Ridgemark Country Club—Diablo
16.	82	DeLaveaga Golf Course
17.	81	Harding Park Golf Course
18.	81	Aptos Seascape Golf Course
19.	80	Fall River Valley Golf & Country Club
20.	80	Rancho Murieta Country Club—South
21.	80	Crystal Springs Golf Club

GOOD

RANK	QUALITY	GOLF COURSE
22.	78	Boundary Oak Golf Course

RANK	QUALITY	GOLF COURSE
23.	77	Pajaro Valley Golf Club
24.	76	Pine Mountain Lake Country Club
25.	76	Ridgemark Country Club—Gabilan
26.	75	Laguna Seca Golf Club
27.	75	Franklin Canyon Golf Course
28.	75	Rancho Cañada Golf Club—East
29.	73	Santa Teresa Golf Club
30.	73	Napa Municipal Golf Course (Kennedy)
31.	72	Fig Garden Golf Club
32.	71	Graeagle Meadows Golf Course
33.	70	Rancho Cañada Golf Club—West
34.	70	Mace Meadows Golf & Country Club
35.	69	Shoreline Golf Course
36.	69	Lake Tahoe Country Club
37.	67	Ancil Hoffman Golf Course
38.	67	Santa Clara Golf & Tennis Club
39.	65	Palo Alto Municipal Golf Course
40.	64	Tilden Park Golf Course
41.	64	Northstar at Tahoe Resort Golf Course
42.	63	La Contenta Golf & Country Club
43.	63	Tularcitos Golf and Country Club
44.	63	Wilcox Oaks Golf Club
45.	61	Indian Valley Golf Club
46.	60	Lake Chabot Golf Course
47.	60	Plumas Pines Country Club

AVERAGE

RANK	QUALITY	GOLF COURSE
48.	59	Gold Hills Golf Club
49.	57	Diamond Oaks Municipal Golf Course
50	57	Salinas Fairways Golf Course
51.	55	Sharp Park Golf Course
52	54	Riverside Golf Course—Coyote
53.	54	Mountain Shadows Golf Course—North
54.	54	Manteca Park Golf Course
55.	54	Blue Rock Springs Municipal Golf Course
56.	53	Haggin Oaks Golf Course—South
57.	53	Bennett Valley Golf Course
58.	53	Alameda Golf Club—Earl Fry
59.	53	Bidwell Park Golf Course
60.	52	Plumas Lake Golf & Country Club
61.	52	Beau Pre Golf Club
62.	52	Riverside Golf Course—Fresno
63.	51	Skywest Golf Course
64.	51	Pacific Grove Municipal Golf Course
65.	51	Willow Park Golf Course
66.	51	Sherwood Forest Golf Club
67.	50	Dry Creek Golf Course
68.	49	San Leandro Tony Lema Golf Course
69.	49	San Jose Municipal Golf Course
70.	48	Rancho Del Rey Golf Club
71	47	Spring Hills Golf Club

RANK	QUALITY	GOLF COURSE
72.	47	Valley Oaks Golf Course
73.	47	Fresno West Golf & Country Club
74.	47	Bishop Country Club
75.	46	Sunnyvale Municipal Golf Course
76.	45	Alta Sierra Golf & Country Club
77.	45	Sonoma National Golf Club
78.	45	Van Buskirk Park Golf Course
79.	45	Las Positas Golf Course
80.	44	Bing Maloney Golf Course
81.	43	Del Monte Golf Course
82.	43	Sunol Valley Golf Club—Cypress
83.	43	Mountain Shadows Golf Course—South
84.	42	Ukiah Municipal Golf Course
85.	41	Sunol Valley Golf Club—Palm
86.	41	San Ramon Royal Vista Golf Club
87.	41	Tulare Golf Club
88.	40	Dryden Park Municipal Golf Course
89.	40	Lincoln Park Golf Course

BELOW AVERAGE

RANK	QUALITY	GOLF COURSE
90.	39	Swenson Park Golf Course
91.	39	Oak Ridge Golf Club
92.	39	Alameda Golf Club
93.	38	Selma Valley Golf Course
94.	33	Eureka Municipal Golf Course
95.	33	Riverbend Golf & Country Club
96.	33	Hidden Valley Golf & Country Club
97.	32	Peacock Gap Golf & Country Club
98.	31	Haggin Oaks Golf Course—Red/Blue
99.	30	Spring Valley Golf Course
100.	30	Diablo Creek Golf Course
101.	29	Fairway Glenn Golf Course
102.	29	Table Mountain Golf Course
103.	28	San Mateo Golf Course
104.	27	Lake Don Pedro Golf & Country Club
105.	27	Sierra View Golf Course
106.	26	Pleasant Hills Golf & Country Club
107.	26	Bethel Island Golf Course
108.	25	Airways Public Golf Course

POOR

RANK	QUALITY	GOLF COURSE
109.	19	Lone Tree Golf Course
110.	17	Lew F. Galbraith Golf Course
111.	11	Green Tree Golf Course
112.	9	Jackson Lakes Golf Course

ZONE QUALITY RANKINGS

SAN FRANCISCO BAY AREA

RANK	QUALITY	GOLF COURSE
1.	98	Canyon Lakes Country Club
2.	96	Fountaingrove Country Club
3.	94	Chardonnay Club
4.	90	Half Moon Bay Golf Links
5.	88	Oakmont Golf Course—West
6.	85	Bodega Harbour Golf Links
7.	81	Harding Park Golf Course
8.	80	Crystal Springs Golf Club
9.	78	Boundary Oak Golf Course
10.	75	Franklin Canyon Golf Course
11.	73	Santa Teresa Golf Club
12.	73	Napa Municipal Golf Course (Kennedy)
13.	69	Shoreline Golf Course
14.	67	Santa Clara Golf & Tennis Club
15.	65	Palo Alto Municipal Golf Course
16.	64	Tilden Park Golf Course
17.	63	Tularcitos Golf and Country Club
18.	61	Indian Valley Golf Club
19.	60	Lake Chabot Golf Course
20.	55	Sharp Park Golf Course
21.	54	Riverside Golf Course—Coyote
22.	54	Mountain Shadows Golf Course—North
23.	54	Blue Rock Springs Municipal Golf Course
24.	53	Bennett Valley Golf Course
25.	53	Alameda Golf Club—Earl Fry
26.	51	Skywest Golf Course
27.	51	Willow Park Golf Course
28.	49	San Leandro Tony Lema Golf Course
29.	49	San Jose Municipal Golf Course
30.	46	Sunnyvale Municipal Golf Course
31.	45	Sonoma National Golf Club

SAN FRANCISCO BAY AREA (cont'd)

RANK	QUALITY	GOLF COURSE
32.	45	Las Positas Golf Course
33.	43	Sunol Valley Golf Club—Cypress
34.	43	Mountain Shadows Golf Course—South
35.	41	Sunol Valley Golf Club—Palm
36.	41	San Ramon Royal Vista Golf Club
37.	40	Lincoln Park Golf Course
38.	39	Oak Ridge Golf Club
39.	39	Alameda Golf Club—Jack Clark
40.	32	Peacock Gap Golf & Country Club
41.	30	Spring Valley Golf Course
42.	30	Diablo Creek Golf Course
43.	29	Fairway Glenn Golf Course
44.	28	San Mateo Golf Course
45.	26	Pleasant Hills Golf & Country Club
46.	19	Lone Tree Golf Course
47.	17	Lew F. Galbraith Golf Course

CENTRAL COAST

RANK	QUALITY	GOLF COURSE
1.	100	Spyglass Hill Golf Course
2.	99	Poppy Hills Golf Course
3.	98	Pebble Beach Golf Course
4.	94	Pasatiempo Golf Club
5.	92	The Links at Spanish Bay
6.	83	Ridgemark Country Club—Diablo
7.	82	DeLaveaga Golf Course
8.	81	Aptos Seascape Golf Course
9.	77	Pajaro Valley Golf Club
10.	76	Ridgemark Country Club—Gabilan
11.	75	Laguna Seca Golf Club
12.	75	Rancho Cañada Golf Club—East
13.	70	Rancho Cañada Golf Club—West
14.	57	Salinas Fairways Golf Club
15.	51	Pacific Grove Municipal Golf Course
16.	47	Spring Hills Golf Club
17.	43	Del Monte Golf Course

CENTRAL VALLEY

RANK	QUALITY	GOLF COURSE
1.	72	Fig Garden Golf Club
2.	67	Ancil Hoffman Golf Course
3.	63	Wilcox Oaks Golf Club
4.	59	Gold Hills Golf Club
5.	57	Diamond Oaks Municipal Golf Course
6.	54	Manteca Park Golf Course
7.	53	Haggin Oaks Golf Course—South
8.	53	Bidwell Park Golf Course

9.	52	Plumas Lake Golf & Country Club
10.	52	Riverside Golf Course—Fresno
11.	51	Sherwood Forest Golf Club
12.	50	Dry Creek Golf Course
13.	48	Rancho Del Rey Golf Club
14.	47	Valley Oaks Golf Course
15.	47	Fresno West Golf & Country Club
16.	45	Van Buskirk Park Golf Course
17.	44	Bing Maloney Golf Course
18.	41	Tulare Golf Club
19.	40	Dryden Park Municipal Golf Course
20.	39	Swenson Park Golf Course
21.	38	Selma Valley Golf Course
22.	33	Riverbend Golf & Country Club
23.	31	Haggin Oaks Golf Course—Red/Blue
24.	29	Table Mountain Golf Course
25.	27	Sierra View Golf Course
26.	26	Bethel Island Golf Course
27.	25	Airways Public Golf Course
28.	11	Green Tree Golf Course
29.	9	Jackson Lakes Golf Course

SIERRA NEVADA MOUNTAINS

RANK	QUALITY	GOLF COURSE
1.	93	Rancho Murieta Country Club—North
2.	89	Lake Shastina Golf Resort
3.	87	Tahoe Donner Golf & Country Club
4.	80	Fall River Valley Golf & Country Club
5.	80	Rancho Murieta Country Club—South
6.	76	Pine Mountain Lake Country Club
7.	71	Graeagle Meadows Golf Course
8.	70	Mace Meadows Golf & Country Club
9.	69	Lake Tahoe Country Club
10.	64	Northstar at Tahoe Resort Golf Course
11.	63	La Contenta Golf & Country Club
12.	60	Plumas Pines Country Club
13.	47	Bishop Country Club
14.	45	Alta Sierra Golf & Country Club
15.	27	Lake Don Pedro Golf & Country Club

NORTH COAST

RANK	QUALITY	GOLF COURSE
1.	52	Beau Pre Golf Club
2.	42	Ukiah Municipal Golf Course
3.	33	Eureka Municipal Golf Course
4.	33	Hidden Valley Golf & Country Club

MUNI/COUNTY—INDEPENDENT
—RESORT QUALITY RANKINGS

MUNI/COUNTY

RANK	QUALITY	GOLF COURSE
1.	82	DeLaveaga Golf Course
2.	81	Harding Park Golf Course
3.	78	Boundary Oak Golf Course
4.	73	Santa Teresa Golf Club
5.	73	Napa Municipal Golf Course (Kennedy)
6.	67	Ancil Hoffman Golf Course
7.	67	Santa Clara Golf & Tennis Club
8.	65	Palo Alto Municipal Golf Course
9.	60	Lake Chabot Golf Course
10.	57	Diamond Oaks Municipal Golf Course
11.	57	Salinas Fairways Golf Course
12	55	Sharp Park Golf Course
13.	54	Mountain Shadows Golf Course—North
14.	54	Manteca Park Golf Course
15.	54	Blue Rock Springs Golf Course
16.	53	Haggin Oaks Golf Course—South
17.	53	Bennett Valley Golf Course
18.	53	Alameda Golf Club—Earl Fry
19.	53	Bidwell Park Golf Course
20.	52	Riverside Golf Course—Fresno
21.	51	Pacific Grove Municipal Golf Course
22.	49	San Leandro Tony Lema Golf Course
23.	49	San Jose Municipal Golf Course
24.	47	Valley Oaks Golf Course
25.	46	Sunnyvale Municipal Golf Course
26.	45	Van Buskirk Park Golf Course
27.	45	Las Positas Golf Course
28.	44	Bing Maloney Golf Course
29.	43	Mountain Shadows Golf Course—South

MUNI/COUNTY (cont'd)

RANK	QUALITY	GOLF COURSE
30.	42	Ukiah Municipal Golf Course
31.	41	Tulare Golf Club
32.	40	Dryden Park Municipal Golf Course
33.	40	Lincoln Park Golf Course
34.	39	Swenson Park Golf Course
35.	39	Alameda Golf Club—Jack Clark
36.	33	Eureka Municipal Golf Course
37.	31	Haggin Oaks Golf Course—Red/Blue
38.	30	Spring Valley Golf Course
39.	30	Diablo Creek Golf Course
40.	29	Fairway Glenn Golf Course
41.	28	San Mateo Golf Course
42.	25	Airways Public Golf Course
43.	19	Lone Tree Golf Course
44.	17	Lew F. Galbraith Golf Course

INDEPENDENT

RANK	QUALITY	GOLF COURSE
1.	99	Poppy Hills Golf Course
2.	98	Canyon Lakes Country Club
3.	96	Fountaingrove Country Club
4.	94	Pasatiempo Golf Club
5.	94	Chardonnay Club
6.	90	Half Moon Bay Golf Links
7.	88	Oakmont Golf Course—West
8.	87	Tahoe Donner Golf & Country Club
9.	85	Bodega Harbour Golf Links
10.	81	Aptos Seascape Golf Course
11.	80	Fall River Valley Golf & Country Club
12.	80	Crystal Springs Golf Club
13.	77	Pajaro Valley Golf Club
14.	75	Laguna Seca Golf Club
15.	75	Franklin Canyon Golf Course
16.	75	Rancho Cañada Golf Club—East
17.	72	Fig Garden Golf Club
18.	71	Graeagle Meadows Golf Course
19.	70	Rancho Cañada Golf Club—West
20.	70	Mace Meadows Golf & Country Club
21.	69	Shoreline Golf Course
22.	69	Lake Tahoe Country Club
23.	64	Tilden Park Golf Course
24.	63	La Contenta Golf & Country Club
25.	63	Tularcitos Golf and Country Club
26.	63	Wilcox Oaks Golf Club
27.	61	Indian Valley Golf Club
28.	60	Plumas Pines Country Club
29.	59	Gold Hills Golf Club
30.	54	Riverside Golf Course—Coyote
31.	52	Plumas Lake Golf & Country Club
32.	52	Beau Pre Golf Club
33.	51	Skywest Golf Course

34.	51	Willow Park Golf Course
35.	51	Sherwood Forest Golf Club
36.	50	Dry Creek Golf Course
37.	48	Rancho Del Rey Golf Club
38.	47	Spring Hills Golf Club
39.	47	Fresno West Golf & Country Club
40.	47	Bishop Country Club
41.	45	Alta Sierra Golf & Country Club
42.	45	Sonoma National Golf Club
43.	43	Sunol Valley Golf Club—Cypress
44.	41	Sunol Valley Golf Club—Palm
45.	41	San Ramon Royal Vista Golf Club
46.	39	Oak Ridge Golf Club
47.	38	Selma Valley Golf Course
48.	33	Riverbend Golf & Country Club
49.	33	Hidden Valley Golf & Country Club
50.	32	Peacock Gap Golf & Country Club
51.	29	Table Mountain Golf Course
52.	27	Lake Don Pedro Golf & Country Club
53.	27	Sierra View Golf Course
54.	26	Pleasant Hills Golf & Country Club
55.	26	Bethel Island Golf Course
56.	11	Green Tree Golf Course
57.	9	Jackson Lakes Golf Course

RESORT

RANK	QUALITY	GOLF COURSE
1.	100	Spyglass Hill Golf Course
2.	98	Pebble Beach Golf Links
3.	93	Rancho Murieta Country Club—North
4.	92	The Links at Spanish Bay
5.	89	Lake Shastina Golf Resort
6.	83	Ridgemark Country Club—Diablo
7.	80	Rancho Murieta Country Club—South
8.	76	Pine Mountain Lake Country Club
9.	76	Ridgemark Country Club—Gabilan
10.	64	Northstar at Tahoe Resort Golf Course
11.	43	Del Monte Golf Course

GREEN FEE QUALITY RANKINGS

$5

RANK	QUALITY	GOLF COURSE
1.	9	Jackson Lakes

$6—$6.50

RANK	QUALITY	GOLF COURSE
1.	57	Diamond Oaks
2.	52	Riverside—Fresno
3.	45	Van Buskirk Park
4.	40	Dryden Park
5.	39	Swenson Park
6.	33	Eureka Municipal
7.	25	Airways Public
8.	19	Lone Tree

$7—$7.50

RANK	QUALITY	GOLF COURSE
1.	54	Manteca
2.	53	Bennett Valley
3.	53	Alameda—Earl Fry
4.	42	Ukiah
5.	39	Alameda—Jack Clark
6.	27	Sierra View
7.	26	Bethel Island
8.	11	Green Tree

$8—$8.50

RANK	QUALITY	GOLF COURSE
1.	55	Sharp Park
2.	54	Blue Rock Springs
3.	53	Haggin Oaks—South
4.	53	Bidwell Park
5.	49	San Leandro Tony Lema

$8—$8.50 (cont'd)

RANK	QUALITY	GOLF COURSE
6.	47	Valley Oaks
7.	47	Fresno West
8.	44	Bing Maloney
9.	43	Mountain Shadows—South
10.	41	Tulare
11.	40	Lincoln Park
12.	31	Haggin Oaks—Red/Blue
13.	29	Table Mountain
14.	28	San Mateo
15.	27	Lake Don Pedro
16.	17	Lew F. Galbraith

$9—$9.50

RANK	QUALITY	GOLF COURSE
1.	73	Napa (Kennedy)
2.	67	Ancil Hoffman
3.	65	Palo Alto
4.	64	Tilden Park
5.	60	Lake Chabot
6.	52	Ukiah
7.	51	Sherwood Forest
8.	46	Sunnyvale
9.	38	Selma Valley
10.	30	Diablo Creek
11.	29	Fairway Glenn

$10

RANK	QUALITY	GOLF COURSE
1.	81	Harding Park
2.	80	Fall River Valley
3.	78	Boundary Oak

$10 (cont'd)

RANK	QUALITY	GOLF COURSE
4.	70	Mace Meadows
5.	63	La Contenta
6.	59	Gold Hills
7.	57	Salinas Fairways
8.	54	Mountain Shadows—South
9.	51	Skywest
10.	47	Spring Hills
11.	45	Las Positas
12.	41	San Ramon Royal Vista
13.	33	Hidden Valley

$11

RANK	QUALITY	GOLF COURSE
1.	51	Willow Park
2.	50	Dry Creek
3.	49	San Jose
4.	45	Sonoma National
5.	26	Pleasant Hills

$12

RANK	QUALITY	GOLF COURSE
1.	75	Franklin Canyon
2.	67	Santa Clara
3.	54	Riverside—Coyote
4.	52	Plumas Lake
5.	51	Pacific Grove
6.	48	Rancho Del Rey
7.	30	Spring Valley

$13

RANK	QUALITY	GOLF COURSE
1.	39	Oak Ridge
2.	33	Riverbend

$14

RANK	QUALITY	GOLF COURSE
1.	73	Santa Teresa
2.	63	Tularcitos
3.	47	Bishop

$15—$15.75

RANK	QUALITY	GOLF COURSE
1.	88	Oakmont—West
2.	83	Ridgemark—Diablo
3.	82	DeLaveaga
4.	76	Ridgemark—Gabilan
5.	72	Fig Garden
6.	63	Wilcox Oaks
7.	61	Indian Valley

$17

RANK	QUALITY	GOLF COURSE
1.	71	Graeagle Meadows
2.	45	Alta Sierra

$20

RANK	QUALITY	GOLF COURSE
1.	81	Aptos Seascape
2.	76	Pine Mountain Lake
3.	43	Sunol Valley—Cypress
4.	41	Sunol Valley—Palm
5.	32	Peacock

$22—$23

RANK	QUALITY	GOLF COURSE
1.	96	Fountaingrove
2.	69	Lake Tahoe

$25—$30

RANK	QUALITY	GOLF COURSE
1.	98	Canyon Lakes
2.	94	Chardonnay
3.	89	Lake Shastina
4.	85	Bodega Harbour
5.	80	Crystal Springs
6.	77	Pajaro Valley
7.	75	Laguna Seca
8.	69	Shoreline
9.	64	Northstar at Tahoe Resort
10.	60	Plumas Pines
11.	43	Del Monte

$34—$45

RANK	QUALITY	GOLF COURSE
1.	94	Pasatiempo
2.	90	Half Moon Bay
3.	87	Tahoe Donner
4.	75	Rancho Cañada—East
5.	70	Rancho Cañada—West

$55 +

RANK	QUALITY	GOLF COURSE
1.	100	Spyglass Hill
2.	99	Poppy Hills
3.	98	Pebble Beach
4.	93	Rancho Murieta—North
5.	92	The Links at Spanish Bay
6.	80	Rancho Murieta—South

NORTHERN CALIFORNIA'S VALUE RANKINGS

A

RANK	VALUE	QUALITY	GOLF COURSE
1.	40.5	81	Harding Park Golf Course
2.	40.0	80	Fall River Valley Golf & Country Club
3.	32.4	73	Napa Municipal Golf Course (Kennedy)
4.	31.2	78	Boundary Oak Golf Course
5.	29.3	88	Oakmont Golf Course—West
6.	28.9	65	Palo Alto Municipal Golf Course
7.	28.4	64	Tilden Park Golf Course
8.	28.2	67	Ancil Hoffman Golf Course
9.	28.0	70	Mace Meadows Golf & Country Club
10.	27.7	83	Ridgemark Country Club—Diablo

B

RANK	VALUE	QUALITY	GOLF COURSE
11.	26.7	60	Lake Chabot Golf Course
12.	26.3	57	Diamond Oaks Municipal Golf Course
13.	26.2	96	Fountaingrove Country Club
14.	26.0	82	DeLaveaga Golf Course
15.	26.0	52	Riverside Golf Course—Fresno
16.	25.2	63	La Contenta Golf & Country Club
17.	25.0	75	Franklin Canyon Golf Course
18.	23.5	98	Canyon Lakes Country Club
19.	22.7	53	Alameda Golf Club—Earl Fry
20.	22.7	53	Bennett Valley Golf Course
21.	22.5	81	Aptos Seascape Golf Course
22.	22.3	67	Santa Clara Golf & Tennis Club
23.	21.6	54	Manteca Park Golf Course
24.	20.9	73	Santa Teresa Golf Club

25.	20.8	45	Van Buskirk Park Golf Course
26.	20.6	55	Sharp Park Golf Course
27.	20.3	76	Ridgemark Country Club—Gabilan
28.	20.3	54	Blue Rock Springs Municipal Golf Course
29.	20.0	40	Dryden Park Municipal Golf Course
30.	19.2	72	Fig Garden Golf Club
31.	18.7	53	Haggin Oaks Golf Course—South
32.	18.7	53	Bidwell Park Golf Course
33.	18.0	42	Ukiah Municipal Golf Course
34.	18.0	63	Tularcitos Golf and Country Club

C

RANK	VALUE	QUALITY	GOLF COURSE
35.	17.6	47	Valley Oaks Golf Course
36.	17.3	52	Beau Pre Golf Club
37.	17.3	49	San Leandro Tony Lema Golf Course
38.	17.1	57	Salinas Fairways Golf Course
39.	17.0	51	Sherwood Forest Golf Club
40.	16.8	63	Wilcox Oaks Golf Club
41.	16.7	71	Graeagle Meadows Golf Course
42.	16.6	47	Fresno West Golf & Country Club
43.	16.4	85	Bodega Harbour Golf Links
44.	16.3	61	Indian Valley Golf Club
45.	16.2	54	Mountain Shadows Golf Course—North
46.	16.1	43	Mountain Shadows Golf Course—South
47.	16.0	80	Crystal Springs Golf Club
48.	15.9	89	Lake Shastina Golf Resort
49.	15.5	44	Bing Maloney Golf Course
50.	15.4	41	Tulare Golf Club
51.	15.3	51	Skywest Golf Course
52.	15.2	76	Pine Mountain Lake Country Club
53.	15.0	40	Lincoln Park Golf Course
54.	14.8	59	Gold Hills Golf Club
55.	14.5	46	Sunnyvale Municipal Golf Course
56.	14.1	47	Spring Hills Golf Club
57.	14.1	94	Chardonnay Club
58.	13.9	51	Willow Park Golf Course
59.	13.6	50	Dry Creek Golf Course
60.	13.5	54	Riverside Golf Course—Coyote
61.	13.5	45	Las Positas Golf Course
62.	13.4	49	San Jose Municipal Golf Course
63.	13.0	52	Plumas Lake Golf Course & Country Club
64.	12.8	87	Tahoe Donner Golf & Country Club
65.	12.8	51	Pacific Grove Municipal Golf Course
66.	12.5	94	Pasatiempo Golf Club
67.	12.3	45	Sonoma National Golf Club
68.	12.0	39	Swenson Park Golf Course
69.	12.0	48	Rancho Del Rey Golf Club
70.	12.0	69	Lake Tahoe Country Club

71.	11.4	77	Pajaro Valley Golf Club
72.	11.3	90	Half Moon Bay Golf Links
73.	11.1	39	Alameda Golf Club—Jack Clark
74.	11.1	75	Laguna Seca Golf Club
75.	11.0	69	Shoreline Golf Course
76.	10.3	41	San Ramon Royal Vista Golf Club
77.	10.2	33	Eureka Municipal Golf Course
78.	10.1	93	Rancho Murieta Country Club—North
79.	10.1	47	Bishop Country Club

D

RANK	VALUE	QUALITY	GOLF COURSE
80.	9.9	99	Poppy Hills Golf Course
81.	9.2	60	Plumas Pines Country Club
82.	8.8	75	Rancho Cañada Golf Club—East
83.	8.5	64	Northstar at Tahoe Resort Golf Course
84.	8.4	38	Selma Valley Golf Course
85.	8.3	25	Airways Public Golf Course
86.	8.2	70	Rancho Cañada Golf Club—West
87.	7.9	45	Alta Sierra Golf & Country Club
88.	7.4	26	Bethel Island Golf Course
89.	7.4	92	The Links at Spanish Bay
90.	7.3	31	Haggin Oaks Golf Course—Red/Blue
91.	7.3	80	Rancho Murieta Country Club—South
92.	7.3	29	Table Mountain Golf Course
93.	7.2	27	Sierra View Golf Course
94.	7.1	100	Spyglass Hill Golf Course
95.	7.0	28	San Mateo Golf Course
96.	6.8	27	Lake Don Pedro Golf & Country Club
97.	6.7	30	Diablo Creek Golf Course
98.	6.6	33	Hidden Valley Golf & Country Club
99.	6.5	43	Sunol Valley Golf Club—Cypress
100.	6.4	29	Fairway Glenn Golf Course
101.	6.2	41	Sunol Valley Golf Club—Palm
102.	6.0	39	Oak Ridge Golf Club

F

RANK	VALUE	QUALITY	GOLF COURSE
103.	5.1	33	Riverbend Golf & Country Club
104.	5.0	30	Spring Valley Golf Course
105.	5.0	43	Del Monte Golf Course
106.	4.7	26	Pleasant Hills Golf & Country Club
107.	4.7	98	Pebble Beach Golf Links
108.	3.2	32	Peacock Gap Golf & Country Club
109.	2.9	19	Lone Tree Golf Course
110.	2.1	17	Lew F. Galbraith Golf Course
111.	1.8	9	Jackson Lakes Golf Course
112.	1.6	11	Green Tree Golf Course

ZONE VALUE RANKINGS

SAN FRANCISCO BAY AREA

RANK	VALUE	QUALITY	GOLF COURSE
1.	40.5	81	Harding Park Golf Course
2.	32.4	73	Napa Municipal Golf Course (Kennedy)
3.	31.2	78	Boundary Oak Golf Course
4.	29.3	88	Oakmont Golf Course—West
5.	28.9	65	Palo Alto Municipal Golf Course
6.	28.4	64	Tilden Park Golf Course
7.	26.7	60	Lake Chabot Golf Course
8.	26.2	96	Fountaingrove Country Club
9.	25.0	75	Franklin Canyon Golf Course
10.	23.5	98	Canyon Lakes Country Club
11.	22.7	53	Alameda Golf Club—Earl Fry
12.	22.7	53	Bennett Valley Golf Course
13.	22.3	67	Santa Clara Golf & Tennis Club
14.	20.9	73	Santa Teresa Golf Club
15.	20.6	55	Sharp Park Golf Course
16.	20.3	54	Blue Rock Springs Municipal Golf Course
17.	18.0	63	Tularcitos Golf and Country Club
18.	17.3	49	San Leandro Tony Lema Golf Course
19.	16.4	85	Bodega Harbour Golf Links
20.	16.3	61	Indian Valley Golf Club
21.	16.2	54	Mountain Shadows Golf Course—North
22.	16.1	43	Mountain Shadows Golf Course—South
23.	16.0	80	Crystal Springs Golf Club
24.	15.3	51	Skywest Golf Course
25.	15.0	40	Lincoln Park Golf Course
26.	14.5	46	Sunnyvale Municipal Golf Course
27.	14.1	94	Chardonnay Club
28.	13.9	51	Willow Park Golf Course
29.	13.5	54	Riverside Golf Course—Coyote
30.	13.5	45	Las Positas Golf Course
31.	13.4	49	San Jose Municipal Golf Course

SAN FRANCISCO BAY AREA (cont'd)

RANK	VALUE	QUALITY	GOLF COURSE
32.	12.3	45	Sonoma National Golf Club
33.	11.3	90	Half Moon Bay Golf Links
34.	11.1	39	Alameda Golf Club—Jack Clark
35.	11.0	69	Shoreline Golf Course
36.	10.3	41	San Ramon Royal Vista Golf Course
37.	7.0	28	San Mateo Golf Course
38.	6.7	30	Diablo Creek Golf Course
39.	6.5	43	Sunol Valley Golf Club—Cypress
40.	6.4	29	Fairway Glenn Golf Course
41.	6.2	41	Sunol Valley Golf Club—Palm
42.	6.0	39	Oak Ridge Golf Club
43.	5.0	30	Spring Valley Golf Course
44.	4.7	26	Pleasant Hills Golf & Country Club
45.	3.2	32	Peacock Gap Golf & Country Club
46.	2.9	19	Lone Tree Golf Course
47.	2.1	17	Lew F. Galbraith Golf Course

CENTRAL COAST

RANK	VALUE	QUALITY	GOLF COURSE
1.	27.7	83	Ridgemark Country Club—Diablo
2.	26.0	82	DeLaveaga Golf Course
3.	22.5	81	Aptos Seascape Golf Course
4.	20.3	76	Ridgemark Country Club—Gabilan
5.	17.1	57	Salinas Fairways Golf Course
6.	14.1	47	Spring Hills Golf Club
7.	12.8	51	Pacific Grove Municipal Golf Course
8.	12.5	94	Pasatiempo Golf Club
9.	11.4	77	Pajaro Valley Golf Club
10.	11.1	75	Laguna Seca Golf Club
11.	9.9	99	Poppy Hills Golf Course
12.	8.8	75	Rancho Cañada Golf Club—East
13.	8.2	70	Rancho Cañada Golf Club—West
14.	7.4	92	The Links at Spanish Bay
15.	7.1	100	Spyglass Hill Golf Course
16.	5.0	43	Del Monte Golf Course
17.	4.7	98	Pebble Beach Golf Links

CENTRAL VALLEY

RANK	VALUE	QUALITY	GOLF COURSE
1.	28.2	67	Ancil Hoffman Golf Course
2.	26.3	57	Diamond Oaks Municipal Golf Course
3.	26.0	52	Riverside Golf Course—Fresno
4.	21.6	54	Manteca Park Golf Course
5.	20.8	45	Van Buskirk Park Golf Course
6.	20.0	40	Dryden Park Municipal Golf Course
7.	19.2	72	Fig Garden Golf Club
8.	18.7	53	Haggin Oaks Golf Course—South
9.	18.7	53	Bidwell Park Golf Course
10.	17.6	47	Valley Oaks Golf Course
11.	17.0	51	Sherwood Forest Golf Club

CENTRAL VALLEY (cont'd)

RANK	VALUE	QUALITY	GOLF COURSE
12.	16.8	63	Wilcox Oaks Golf Club
13.	16.6	47	Fresno West Golf & Country Club
14.	15.5	44	Bing Maloney Golf Course
15.	15.4	41	Tulare Golf Club
16.	14.8	59	Gold Hills Golf Club
17.	13.6	50	Dry Creek Golf Course
18.	13.0	52	Plumas Lake Golf & Country Club
19.	12.0	39	Swenson Park Golf Course
20.	12.0	48	Rancho Del Rey Golf Club
21.	8.4	38	Selma Valley Golf Course
22.	8.3	25	Airways Public Golf Course
23.	7.4	26	Bethel Island Golf Course
24.	7.3	31	Haggin Oaks Golf Course—Red/Blue
25.	7.3	29	Table Mountain Golf Course
26.	7.2	27	Sierra View Golf Course
27.	5.1	33	Riverbend Golf & Country Club
28.	1.8	9	Jackson Lakes Golf Course
29.	1.6	11	Green Tree Golf Course

SIERRA NEVADA MOUNTAINS

RANK	VALUE	QUALITY	GOLF COURSE
1.	40.0	80	Fall River Valley Golf & Country Club
2.	28.0	70	Mace Meadows Golf & Country Club
3.	25.2	63	La Contenta Golf & Country Club
4.	16.7	71	Graeagle Meadows Golf Course
5.	15.9	89	Lake Shastina Golf Resort
6.	15.2	76	Pine Mountain Lake Country Club
7.	12.8	87	Tahoe Donner Golf & Country Club
8.	12.0	69	Lake Tahoe Country Club
9.	10.1	93	Rancho Murieta Country Club—North
10.	10.1	47	Bishop Country Club
11.	9.2	60	Plumas Pines Country Club
12.	8.5	64	Northstar at Tahoe Resort Golf Course
13.	7.9	45	Alta Sierra Country Club
14.	7.3	80	Rancho Murieta Country Club—South
15.	6.8	27	Lake Don Pedro Golf & Country Club

NORTH COAST

RANK	VALUE	QUALITY	GOLF COURSE
1.	18.0	42	Ukiah Municipal Golf Course
2.	17.3	52	Beau Pre Golf Club
3.	10.2	33	Eureka Municipal Golf Course
4.	6.6	33	Hidden Valley Golf & Country Club

TRIVIA ANSWERS

1. Fall River Valley Golf & Country Club (the third hole is 666 yards)
2. Green Tree Golf Course and Pacific Grove Municipal Golf Course
3. Sunol Valley Golf Club, Alameda Golf Club, Haggin Oaks Golf Course, Rancho Cañada Golf Club, Rancho Murieta Country Club, Ridgemark Country Club
4. Pasatiempo Golf Club (16th hole)
5. Poppy Hills Golf Course
6. Fig Garden Golf Club
7. Pine Mountain Lake Country Club
8. Beau Pre Golf Club
9. Pebble Beach Golf Links and Spyglass Hill Golf Course
10. Pine Mountain Lake Country Club (the second hole is 489 yards)
11. Lincoln Park Golf Course
12. Spring Valley Golf Course
13. Dryden Park Municipal Golf Course
14. Diamond Oaks Municipal Golf Course
15. Lake Tahoe Country Club
16. Harding Park Golf Course
17. Lake Don Pedro Golf & Country Club (the seventh hole is 246 yards)
18. Sharp Park Golf Course
19. Spring Hills Golf Club
20. Canyon Lakes Country Club (fourth hole), Jackson Lakes Golf Course (16th hole)
21. Lake Shastina Golf Resort
22. Bodega Harbour Golf Links
23. Northstar at Tahoe Resort Golf Course
24. Gold Hills Golf Club
25. Ancil Hoffman Golf Course
26. Laguna Seca Golf Club
27. La Contenta Golf & Country Club (the 14th hole is 424 yards)
28. Peacock Gap Golf & Country Club
29. Oak Ridge Golf Club, Fairway Glenn Golf Course, Pasatiempo Golf Club, Pacific Grove Municipal Golf Course, Wilcox Oaks Golf Club, Airways Public Golf Course, Lake Don Pedro Golf & Country Club, Eureka Municipal Golf Course
30. Shoreline Golf Course
31. Sunol Valley Golf Club
32. Indian Valley Golf Club
33. Del Monte Golf Course
34. Tilden Park Golf Course, Graeagle Meadows Golf Course, Sherwood Forest Golf Club
35. Van Buskirk Park Golf Course (the 14th hole is 243 yards)
36. Bishop Country Club
37. Rancho Murieta Country Club—North
38. Lake Chabot Golf Course
39. Mace Meadows Golf & Country Club
40. Pacific Grove Municipal Golf Course surrounds Point Pinos Lighthouse
41. Chardonnay Club, #13 (each flag is for championship, regular, women's tee boxes)
42. Diablo Creek Golf Course is across from Concord Naval Weapons Station
43. Lone Tree Golf Course (the 14th hole is 85 yards)
44. Pleasant Hills Golf & Country Club
45. Oak Ridge Golf Club
46. Pebble Beach Golf Links and Half Moon Bay Golf Links
47. Bethel Island Golf Course
48. Lake Chabot Golf Course (the 18th hole, par 6, is 665 yards)
49. ONLY YOU CAN ANSWER THIS QUESTION!

INDEX